The Remarkable Record of JOB

The Ancient Wisdom, Scientific
Accuracy, and Life-changing Message
of an Amazing Book.

The Remarkable Record of JOB

The Ancient Wisdom, Scientific
Accuracy, and Life-changing Message
of an Amazing Book.

Dr. Henry Morris

Master
Books

Master Books edition
First printing: March 2000
Fourth printing: April 2007

ISBN-13: 978-0-89051-292-0
ISBN-10: 0-89051-292-2
Library of Congress Catalog Card Number: 00-100213

Printed in the United States of America

Please visit our website for other great titles:
www.masterbooks.net

Contents

Foreword

The most fascinating book in the Bible" is the title of the first chapter in Dr. Henry Morris's commentary *The Remarkable Record of Job*. Some Bible students might argue that the title should be "the most forgotten book in the Bible." I predict, however, that those who read Dr. Morris's book will agree with his original statement.

Most commentaries on Job emphasize its literary style or attempt to analyze its philosophical content. They usually conclude that the book simply records the utter despair of a godly man (either real or mythical) enduring great suffering as he vainly attempts to find some divine purpose for his pain.

This is *not* the approach taken by Dr. Morris. In nine concise, analytical, and thought-provoking chapters, he reveals that the book of Job . . .

serves as an overview of Satan and his wicked activities.

supports a literal interpretation of Genesis 1–11 and provides additional details.

does *not* deal primarily with the problem of suffering in the lives of godly people.

He concludes that the book has a two-fold purpose. Its heavenly purpose is to demonstrate God's sovereignty to angels (both good and evil) and perhaps to believers already in glory. Its earthly purpose is to re-emphasize the importance of God's original creation. In fact, Morris shows that creation is the basis of true Christology, faith, salvation, fellowship, and peace among human beings.

To my mind, Dr. Morris has written a volume that will become—to rephrase his chapter title—the most fascinating book *on Job*.

Harold L. Willmington

Acknowledgments

I would like to specially thank Dr. Harold L. Willmington for reviewing the manuscript and for writing the Foreword to this book. Dr. Willmington is a long-time friend and a keen Bible student. As Vice President of Liberty University and Director of the University's International Bible Center, Dr. Willmington is a prolific author in his own right, most notably of the widely used *Willmington's Guide to the Bible*. His review and commendation of my latest book is greatly appreciated.

I also thank my daughter, Mrs. Mary Smith, for typing the manuscript and Mrs. Margaret Riedel for suggesting that I undertake this study in the first place. Finally, thanks are certainly in order for the fine editorial and publishing work of Dan Van't Kerkhoff, Betty De Vries, and their colleagues at Baker Book House.

Henry M. Morris
March 1988

1

The Most Fascinating
Book in the Bible

A masterpiece of literature, the Book of Job has intrigued readers for many generations. Though the book is ancient, its insights are remarkably modern, and its message is needed more today than ever before. Its long discourses, though sometimes difficult to follow, and seemingly redundant, sparkle with beautiful poetry and vibrate with deep emotion, thus contributing to the fascination that grips the thoughtful reader. Its insights penetrate human nature, offer foresights into modern science, and probe the very heart of God.

All of this makes the Book of Job what this writer, at least, believes is the most fascinating book in the Bible. The climax of its message, though unexpected, is intensely practical, with special relevance to the needs of God's people in these days of widespread humanism and evolutionary scientism.

Many commentaries, both liberal and conservative, have been written on the Book of Job, but few writers allow the book to speak for itself. Consequently, many expositors read interpretations *into* it rather than derive interpretations *from* it. Job's God-centered message has often been bypassed by writers seeking answers to man-centered problems. It is important to keep in view the heavenly perspective with which it begins and ends. Otherwise, we may become entangled in the introspective humanistic philosophies that God himself eventually repudiates.

The Oldest Book

The Book of Job may also be the oldest book in the Bible, with the probable exception of the first eleven chapters of Genesis. There can, at least, be no question about its setting in the patriarchal period, certainly before Moses and possibly even before Abraham.

The events described in Job obviously took place before the establishment of Israel as God's covenant nation. There is no hint in the book of the nation of Israel—no mention of Moses, or Abraham, or any of the judges, kings, or prophets of Israel. Yet the Book of Job has always been accepted by the children of Israel as one of the canonical books of Scripture.

Even more significant is the fact that there is no mention of the Ten Commandments or any of the Mosaic laws. Many of the discourses in the book center on questions of right and wrong, sin and judgment, reward and punishment, but they never are placed in the context of God's Mount Sinai revelations.

Divine laws were given to men and women long before Moses. Abraham was guided by such laws: "Abraham obeyed my voice, and kept my charge, my commandments, my statutes, and my laws" (Gen. 26:5).

Exactly how these primeval laws were given, and in what form, we do not know, for they have not been preserved.

They have been superseded, first by the Mosaic laws, then also by the law of Christ. They were known by Abraham, however, and no doubt by his ancestors. They were also known by Job, for he testified: "Neither have I gone back from the commandment of his lips; I have esteemed the words of his mouth more than my necessary food" (Job 23:12). Job's friends also were aware of them. Their chief spokesman, Eliphaz, urged Job as follows: "Receive, I pray thee, the law from his mouth, and lay up his words in thine heart" (Job 22:22).

The laws of Moses laid great stress on the sacrificial system and set aside the tribe of Levi to officiate at the sacrifices for the sins of the people. Before this system was established, however, the patriarchal head of each family offered the sacrifices. Note, for example, the practice of Noah and Abraham (Gen. 8:20; 22:13). This was also the practice of Job (Job 1:5) and even of his three friends (Job 42:7–9).

Perhaps the most significant evidence of all, that the story of Job predated the Mosaic laws, is that the almost universal drift of the early nations into pantheistic idolatry after the dispersion at Babel had not yet infected the tribes mentioned in Job. Job, the Uzite, Eliphaz, the Temanite, Bildad, the Shuhite, Zophar, the Naamathite, and Elihu, the Buzite, all believed in the true God of creation. Their concepts of God's ways with man proved inadequate, but none of the men were inclined toward other gods. There is no hint of pantheism, polytheism, idolatry, or evolutionism anywhere in the book, and such a situation is inconceivable anywhere in any nation much after the time of Abraham.

Furthermore, quite a number of references in Job refer to the early events recorded in Genesis—for example, the creation, the fall, the flood, and the dispersion. A number of ancient tribes and places mentioned in Job such as the Sabaeans, the Chaldeans, and Ophir tie into the Table of Nations (Gen. 10) or other early sections of Genesis, but none that characterize later periods.

Job lived 140 years after the events described in the book (Job 42:16). By figuring in the approximate number of years he lived prior to those events (the exact number is unknown, but at least enough to have ten grown children), we can place him in the time of the early patriarchs, perhaps around 2000 B.C.

Job and the Land of Uz

The geographical setting of the book is the land of Uz, but the exact location is uncertain. The Bible mentions two men named Uz. The first was the son of Aram (founder of the Aramaeans), the son of Shem, the son of Noah. The other was a grandson of Seir, the Horite (or Hurrian) who first settled the area later known as Mount Seir, which eventually fell into the hands of Esau and became part of the land of the Edomites (see Gen. 36:8, 20, 21, 28). The second Uz may have been named in memory of the first, who was perhaps his ancestor.

The land of Uz is associated with the land of Edom in Lamentations 4:21: "Rejoice and be glad, O daughter of Edom, that dwellest in the land of Uz." This ascription implies that the land received the name Uz before the Edomites entered it.

In any case, Uz was in or near the region later known as Edom, extending both southwest and southeast of the Dead Sea. Though largely a desert now, in the time of Abraham, and later of Esau, it was apparently well-populated, fertile, and attractive. Job, evidently one of its leading citizens, was highly respected by the princes and nobles of the land (Job 29:7–10), esteemed and loved by everyone except the wicked, who incurred his judgment. Job was "the greatest of all the men of the east" (Job 1:3), and, according to his own testimony, he "dwelt as a king in the army, as one that comforteth the mourners" (Job 29:25).

Who Was Job?

Skeptics and liberals often deny that Job ever lived. To them, the story of Job is pious fiction—a great dramatic poem no doubt, but no more historical than other ancient epics.

This contradicts the acceptance of Job as a true record of events by both the ancient Jews and early Christians. These early authorities surely knew more about this than modern critics who pick apart the Scriptures to conform to their own humanistic biases. The author of Job presents his narrative as a true account, and it would have been blasphemous for him to describe events taking place in heaven and to devote four chapters to a verbatim transcription of God's words if it were merely a vehicle for him to present his own philosophy.

Furthermore, the prophet Ezekiel, during the exile, characterized Job along with Noah and Daniel as historical paragons of righteousness (Ezek. 14:14, 20). James, in the New Testament, also cited Job as an exemplary character: "Ye have heard of the patience of Job, and have seen the end of the Lord; that the Lord is very pitiful, and of tender mercy" (James 5:11). Divinely inspired writers of both the Old and New Testaments accepted Job as a real person and as a man unsurpassed in righteousness and patience. *Job = persecuted*

The meaning of Job's name is uncertain, but the most commonly accepted meaning is "hated" or "persecuted." One of the sons of Issachar, who came down into Egypt with grandfather Jacob, was also named Job (Gen. 46:13), and several men named Jobab are mentioned in the Bible. One was a king of Edom (Gen. 36:33). None of these, however, lived during the days of the patriarch Job.

Interestingly, Noah lived for 350 years and Shem for 502 years after the great flood (Gen. 9:28; 11:10, 11), so it is possible that Job's life overlapped the lives of these patriarchs. Assuming that the Massoretic text is the closest to the original Old Testament Hebrew manuscripts and that no generations are missing from the chronological and genea-

logical lists of Genesis 11, Abraham was born only 292 years
after the flood. One or both of these assumptions are rejected by many conservative expositors, but nothing is un-
reasonable about either of them.[1]

In any case, Job and his contemporaries knew and worshipped the God of Noah and Shem, even though they were
not in the direct line of promise from Noah to Abraham. In
his discourses, Job shows much knowledge of the primeval
ages described in Genesis 1–11, so apparently he had access
to the same records (though perhaps not in the same form) as
those that Moses later used to compile and edit the early
chapters of Genesis. In fact, he believed and followed God so
fully that God Himself testified: "There is none like him in
the earth, a perfect and an upright man, one that feareth
God, and escheweth evil" (Job 1:8).

Who Wrote Job's Record?

Liberal theologians have often dealt dishonestly with Job,
imagining that it was produced by some unknown writer
during the exile of the Jews in Babylon, around 400 B.C.
There is no basis for such a claim, either internally or
externally, and no ancient theologians, Jewish or Christian,
ever imagined such a thing. Certain portions of Job have
been found among the Dead Sea Scrolls, which date back to
the first century B.C. indicating that Job was an accepted
part of the Old Testament canonical Scriptures long before
that time. The New Testament writers quote from Job just
as they do from other books of the Old Testament (e.g., Job
5:13, quoted in 1 Cor. 3:19).

Many conservative scholars also have undermined Job's
authenticity by attributing it to some writer during the
period of King Solomon. The reason for this is that Job is
usually grouped with Psalms, Proverbs, Ecclesiastes, and

1. For evidence supporting this short chronology, refer to the discussion in
Henry M. Morris, *The Genesis Record* (Grand Rapids: Baker Book House, 1976),
278–90.

Song of Solomon in what they call the "wisdom literature" of the Old Testament. As a great dramatic poem, it obviously fits more conveniently with these four books (which were written or compiled during the Solomonic era) than with the historical or prophetic books, but there is neither internal nor external evidence that it was written at that time. Certain sections of Job are similar to portions of Psalms, Proverbs, and Ecclesiastes, but it is likely that these were influenced by Job, rather than vice versa.

As noted above, its setting, structure, theme, and internal references correspond more to the early chapters of Genesis than to any other section of Scripture. This correlates beautifully with the fact that ancient Jewish tradition has always attributed it to Moses, not to some unknown dramatist of the Solomonic or exile periods.

Furthermore, modern archaeological research supports the probability that Job's author lived no later than the time of Moses, and probably much earlier. The name *Job* has been found in a number of tablets dated 2,000 B.C. (the time of Abraham) or earlier. These include Akkadian documents from Tel-el-Amarna, Mari, and Alalakh, and the Execration Texts from Egypt. The name "Bildad" has also been noted in a cuneiform text from this period. Finally, a number of Sumerian documents incorporate the literary motif of the righteous sufferer.

None of these archaeological references should be taken as referring to the actual Biblical record, of course. Nevertheless, they do confirm the high probability that the biblical account was written sometime in the same general period. Writers of many centuries later could hardly have been aware of these archaeological data.

The tradition of Mosaic authorship of Job should, therefore, be taken quite seriously, but in the same sense that the first eleven chapters of Genesis are ascribed to Moses. The events in both these records took place long before Moses' time, so he would necessarily have to draw on earlier records. In the case of Genesis 1–11, the evidence is quite strong that tablets written by the ancient patriarchs were handed down from Adam to Noah to Shem and so on, finally to be compiled and edited by Moses.[2]

In somewhat the same fashion, Moses must have obtained the tablets recounting Job's experiences, recognizing them as a supremely important revelation of God's dealings with all men, even with those outside his covenant relationship with Abraham, Isaac, and Jacob. Then, in the way he incorporated Genesis along with his personal writings in the other four books of the Pentateuch, he prepared the Book of Job for later generations of Israelites, who soon recognized it as inspired Scripture.

As to when Moses did this, it is probable that he acquired the documents during his forty-year exile in Midian (Acts 7:23, 30), which is near Edom and Uz. It is possible that Moses met some of Job's children or grandchildren during this time and persuaded them to part with the Joban tablets. From them, Moses could have learned more about God and perhaps more insight on the persecutions he and the people of Israel were experiencing. He also could have used them to instruct the Israelites later. He probably would not have had access at this time to the Genesis documents, which had been handed down through Jacob and were presumably in safekeeping in the land of Goshen, where the children of Israel were dwelling. Later he would see these and learn how beautifully they complemented the Book of Job.

The above scenario is speculative, but it is more reasonable than the speculations of those who think Job was written many centuries after Moses. The firm Jewish tradition associating Moses with the Book of Job did not spring out of thin air.

This still does not settle the ultimate authorship. Just as in Genesis, the Book of Job, with its detailed discourses,

2. Ibid. 22–30. This concept was first elaborated by P.J. Wiseman in his *New Discoveries in Babylonia about Genesis* (London: Marshall, Morgan and Scott, 1946), 143.

could only have been written by an eye-witness. The conversations must either have been recorded at the time or else
supernaturally recalled to mind (in the manner promised by
Christ to his disciples concerning his own discourses—note
John 14:26) to be recorded in their entirety.

Therefore, the original author of the Book of Job must
have been Job himself, who wrote as inspired by the Holy
Spirit (2 Tim. 3:16), faithfully reproducing the original
events and conversations. Parts of the Prologue (Job 1:6–12;
2:1–7) must have been specially revealed by God, either to
Job or later to Moses as he edited.

Job's authorship is strongly suggested in his heartfelt cry
at the height of his sufferings: "Oh that my words were now
written! oh that they were printed in a book! That they were
graven with an iron pen and lead in the rock for ever!" (Job
19:23–24). Once his sufferings were over and both he and
God had been vindicated to both Satan and the whole world,
surely Job would return to write down all the details of his
remarkable experiences.

This is what we have in this fascinating Book of Job! The
eye-witness account of a man who experienced both suffering and blessing in tremendous measure and who had a
direct encounter of incomparable significance with God
himself. We do well to learn from it, for it offers great and
immediate application to our own lives.

Surveying the Book

This book is not a verse-by-verse commentary of Job because many of the views expressed by Job contradict those
of his friends, so both cannot be true. All the discourses are
divinely inspired in the sense of being correctly reported,
but they often illumine the faulty reasonings and attitudes
of fallible human beings rather than the inerrant revelations
of an infallible God. Also, because most expositors of Job
have either ignored or misunderstood its scientific insights
and its references to the primeval ages, this discussion will

focus as much on these aspects of the Book of Job as on its philosophical and theological implications. The latter will not be ignored, however, as they have often been misinterpreted by those who fail to place the book in its scientific and historical contexts.

This study will treat the book as a self-consistent whole, ignoring the unsupported and subjective contentions of critics who say that parts of it (e.g., the prologue, Elihu's discourse, God's climactic message, and the epilogue) represent later additions. The following general outline of its major internal subdivisions helps to give an overview of the whole book.

1. *Prologue (chapters 1–2)*. An introduction to Job and his circumstances is followed by the heavenly dialogue between God and Satan, culminating in the calamities that caused Job's terrible sufferings and the arrival of three friends to "comfort" him.

2. *Job's Cry of Misery and Despair (chapter 3)*.

3. *First Round of Discourses (chapters 4–14)*. Eliphaz (from Teman, an ancient city later prominent in Edom), Bildad (from Shuhu, an Aramaean city south of Haran, on the middle Euphrates), and Zophar (from Naamah, a city believed to be in Arabia or possibly in Edom) discuss Job's plight. Each elicits a defensive response from Job. The friends attribute Job's sufferings to God's punishment of some hidden sin; Job insists he is innocent.

4. *Second Round of Discourses (chapters 15–21)*. Job and his friends continue to argue the same themes—the friends stress guilt and punishment; Job claims innocence and mystification—though more briefly.

5. *Third Round of Discourses (chapters 22–31)*. Eliphaz speaks even more briefly; Job answers; then Bildad speaks briefly. Zophar remains silent. Job, still insisting he is innocent of known sin, follows with an extensive, summarizing statement.

6. *Elihu's Discourse (chapters 32–37)*. A young man named Elihu (from Buz, probably in northern Arabia) intervenes

with an extended and opinionated monologue, contending that he can set straight both Job and his friends. He has little to add, however, that is substantive and nonrepetitious. Job does not answer him, since he introduced nothing new.

7. *God's Challenge (chapters 38–41).* Finally God speaks to the entire group, especially to Job, out of a great whirlwind. He rebukes Elihu first, then the other three. The major portion of his divine challenge consists of a great exposition of his creation—first physical, then biological. After a brief respite, his message climaxes in a remarkable description of two great animals, Behemoth and Leviathan.

8. *Epilogue (chapter 42).* Job acknowledges his own unworthiness. God continues to speak, vindicating Job but requiring him to pray for his friends after their own repentance and sacrificial offering. Finally Job is restored to health and prosperity and given a large family and long life.

As we read Job, we need to keep in mind that not all statements—with the exception of God's own words in chapters 38–42)—necessarily express divine truth, but all are correctly recorded by divine inspiration. On the other hand, many statements do indeed contain important truths, sometimes even brilliant scientific insights far ahead of their time, and spiritual truths confirmed and elaborated in later biblical revelation. Each passage must be evaluated on its own merits, in its own context, and in the broader context of Scripture as a whole. Even those statements that must be rejected as untrue or insufficiently true (e.g., claims that suffering is always a symptom of guilt) help us understand human nature or some other aspect of truth, which does, indeed, make it "profitable" for study. "All Scripture is given by inspiration of God, and is profitable" (2 Tim. 3:16). This is true of every verse in Job, even though our specific purpose in this study is not a verse-by-verse exposition.

The Misunderstood Purpose of Job

Unfortunately, many expositors maintain that the main theme in Job is the mystery of suffering: "Why do the righteous suffer?" Why does a God who is omnipotent (thus *able* to prevent suffering) and merciful (thus *willing* to prevent suffering) *allow* suffering, particularly in the lives of those who have done nothing to deserve it? This problem is a major weapon in the atheist's arsenal and thus is a major theme of numerous books in Christian apologetics.

But it is *not* the major theme of the Book of Job! With all due respect to the many capable and godly preachers and writers who have taught that this is the major question addressed in Job, we still have to note that if this *is* the question, it is never answered in the Book of Job.

It is not answered by the fact that Job is finally restored and made more prosperous than ever. Many godly Christians go through suffering without any such restoration. Many have even been martyred. Think of the apostle Paul, for example!

Nor is it answered in terms of the future life. Multitudes have died outside of Christ, and thus with no promise of heaven, whose tremendous suffering on earth had no obvious cause-and-effect relation to previous sins. On the other hand, many blatantly sinful men and women have enjoyed health, prosperity, and long lives.

Scripture deals with these problems, but they are not answered in the Book of Job, though suffering is discussed at great length by Job and his friends. The friends insist on a patently wrong answer, and Job acknowledges he doesn't know the answer. When God finally stops their philosophizing, he doesn't give the answer either! He does not even mention the subject in his four-chapter discourse, which would be strange if the question of unmerited suffering is God's reason for including the Book of Job in the Holy Scriptures.

But if this is not its purpose, what is? To understand and appreciate the purpose we need to explore more fully the remarkable scientific and historical data scattered throughout the book, especially in the climactic sermon of God in its final chapters.

2

Reflections of Primeval History

In light of the antiquity of the Book of Job, it is not surprising that it includes many references to the great events associated with the earth's primeval ages. Conversely, these references may be cited as evidence for the book's antiquity. They are not listed as a recitation of history, but are mentioned only in passing. This argues both for the historicity of the events and for the antiquity of the book itself. They are mentioned almost casually, suggesting that they were common knowledge at the time of writing, with no need to stress their historicity. The spreading system of pagan pantheism, with its underlying premise of long, cyclic ages and evolutionary changes, which soon infected all the dispersing post-Babel tribes, had apparently not yet made a significant impact on Job and his friends. In this chapter, therefore, references to the ancient histories will be noted, along with their significance, to provide an appropriate background for Job's message.

Creation

The official account of creation was given by God, probably through the first man, Adam, in the first two chapters of Genesis. These great chapters are the foundation of the Bible. Many other references to creation are scattered through the Bible, but none are more intriguing than those in Job.

The Book of Job assumes that God is the creator of all things. There are no references to other gods and no suggestion that the world evolved out of some earlier form, as pagan philosophers taught in ancient times. The creation of the heavens by God, "Which alone spreadeth out the heavens," is noted in Job 9:8. God reminds Job that he "laid the foundations of the earth" (Job 38:4). The establishment of day and night by the rotation of the earth is implied in Job 38:12–14.

Stars were created on the fourth day of creation week (Gen. 1:16), and this is mentioned in Job 9:9: "which maketh Arcturus, Orion, and Pleiades, and the chambers of the south." Note also Job 26:13: "By his spirit he hath garnished the heavens."

The creation of animals is the theme of the following classic passage: "But ask now the beasts, and they shall teach thee; and the fowls of the air, and they shall tell thee: Or speak to the earth, and it shall teach thee: and the fishes of the sea shall declare unto thee. Who knoweth not in all these that the hand of the LORD hath wrought this? In whose hand is the soul of every living thing, and the breath of all mankind" (Job 12:7–10).

The latter verse reflects Genesis 1:21: "God created great whales, and every living creature (same as living soul)." It also reflects Genesis 2:7: "And the LORD God formed man of the dust of the ground, and breathed into his nostrils the breath of life; and man became a living soul." The word *breath* is often the same in the Hebrew as *spirit*, and it is recognized in Job that man has both "soul" and "spirit." In his discourse, Elihu refers to this verse: "The Spirit of God (same as 'breath of God') hath made me, and the breath of the Almighty hath given me life. . . . I also am formed out of the clay" (Job 33:4–6). Note also Job's statement: "All the while my breath is in me, and the spirit of God is in my nostrils" (Job 27:3). Adam is even mentioned by name in Job 31:33.

It is significant also that God is called "the Almighty" more in Job than in all the rest of the Bible put together. The Hebrew word is *Shaddai*, and some commentators have unfortunately associated this with *shad*, the Hebrew word for *breast*, suggesting that this name stresses his character as the nourisher or even suggesting a female dimension to his nature. The Jews, however, who understood the etymology of their own language better than later Gentile scholars, translated it *pantokrator* in the Greek Septuagint translation of the Old Testament—a word that means almighty and nothing else. Its abundant use in Job still further stresses the recognition of God as the omnipotent Creator by Job and his Semitic contemporaries.

The Fall and the Curse

When Adam and Eve brought sin into the world, God's curse, which included death, soon followed. The impact of this is felt deeply in Job. Elihu, for example, referred to Genesis 3:19 ("unto dust shalt thou return") when he said: "If [God] set his heart upon man, if he gather unto himself his spirit and his breath; All flesh shall perish together, and man shall turn again unto dust" (Job 34:14–15).

The curse on woman and her offspring (Gen. 3:16—"in sorrow thou shalt bring forth children") is alluded to by Job: "Man that is born of a woman is of few days, and full of trouble. He cometh forth like a flower, and is cut down: he fleeth also as a shadow, and continueth not. . . . Who can bring a clean thing out of an unclean? not one" (Job 14:1-4). Eliphaz says: "What is man, that he should be clean? and he which is born of woman, that he should be righteous?" (Job 15:14).

There are still other references to the curse. "Man is born unto trouble, as the sparks fly upward" (Job 5:7). "Remember, I beseech thee, that thou hast made me as the clay: and wilt thou bring me into dust again?" (Job 10:9). "How then can man be justified with God? or how can he be clean that is born of a woman?" (Job 25:4).

Job climaxes all his discourses and his final complaint by referring to the sin of Adam which brought this great curse of God on the earth: "If I covered my transgressions as Adam, by hiding mine iniquity in my bosom" (Job 31:33). He concludes by an implied reference to the specific terms of the curse itself: "Let thistles grow instead of wheat, and cockle instead of barley. The words of Job are ended" (Job 31:40).

The Great Flood

The worldwide flood sent as a judgment from God in the days of Noah was much nearer than the creation to the time of Job, so it is not surprising that there are even more references to the flood than to creation. The chronology is uncertain, but if there are no significant gaps in the chronologies of Genesis 11, it is possible that Job's experience could have occurred only 300 or so years after the flood.

The reason God destroyed the earth and all land animals, except those in the ark, was because "the wickedness of man was great in the earth, and...every imagination of the thoughts of his heart was only evil continually" (Gen. 6:5). Eliphaz, in his third discourse, recalled this fact: "Hast thou marked the old way which wicked men have trodden? Which were cut down out of time, whose foundation was overthrown with a flood: Which said unto God, Depart from us: and what can the Almighty do for them?" (Job 22:15-17).

Evidence for the cataclysmic violence of the flood is found
not only in the Bible but also in geological features all over
the globe. The apostle Peter said: "The world [cosmos] that
then was, being overflowed with water, perished" (2 Peter
3:6). This earth-changing, destructive physical cataclysm
was well-remembered in traditions all over the world, including the ancestral traditions of Job and his friends. In
one of his discourses, Job said: "Behold, he [God] breaketh
down, and it cannot be built again: he shutteth up a man, and
there can be no opening. Behold, he withholdeth the waters,
and they dry up: also he sendeth them out, and they overturn
the earth" (Job 12:14–15).

The words *dry up* probably refer to the "waters...above
the firmament" (Gen. 1:7) that were established on the second day of creation, resulting in a "greenhouse effect" that
made rain impossible in the primeval world (Gen. 2:5). This
global water blanket, probably water vapor, was withheld
from the earth until God used it to "overturn the earth" in
the days of Noah.

"He shutteth up a man, and there can be no opening."
When the appointed time came, Noah went into the ark "as
God had commanded him: and the LORD shut him in" (Gen.
7:16). There was only one "door of the ark" (Gen. 6:16), and it
could not be opened until the earth had been overturned by
the great waters.

The same word, referring to the same great overturning,
occurs also in Job's previous discourse. "[God] removeth the
mountains, and they know not: which overturneth them in
his anger. Which shaketh the earth out of her place, and the
pillars thereof tremble. Which commandeth the sun, and it
riseth not: and sealeth up the stars. Which alone spreadeth
out the heavens, and treadeth upon the waves of the sea"
(Job 9:5–8).

This passage, with verses following, interweaves God's
creative works with the destructive work of the flood. Note
also Job 28:9: "He putteth forth his hand upon the rock; he
overturneth the mountains by the roots." The fountains of

the deep opened, the floodgates of heaven released their torrents, the waters rose higher than the mountains, erosion began to wash away the heights, and soon the roots of the mountains were overturned.

Job 26:11–14 suggests the unparalleled magnitude of the flood and its dual physical triggering phenomenon: "The pillars of heaven tremble and are astonished at his reproof. He divideth the sea with his power, and by his understanding he smiteth through the proud. . . . Lo these are parts of his ways: but how little a portion is heard of him? but the thunder of his power who can understand?"

Though obviously figurative language, it is very realistic. There were no literal pillars holding up the heavens any more than there were literal windows in heaven. Nevertheless, when the torrents of water began to pour down for the first time in history from "the waters which were above the firmament" (Gen. 1:7), it must have seemed that mighty supports restraining the floodgates of the heavenly reservoir had suddenly trembled and given way.

At the same time, the pre-flood seas were divided when the primeval crust opened all over the world and waters sprang out through the broken fountains of the deep. This "dividing" of the sea could not refer to the Red Sea opening up for Moses and the Israelites at the Exodus, for that event took place long after Job had spoken these words. They can only refer to the destruction of the great flood, which, indeed, was the unique time above all past times, when God "by his understanding. . .smiteth through the proud." Yet, as Job said, this is only a small portion of his power. The "thunder of his power" is reserved for a greater day of judgment yet to come.

End of the Flood

The Noahic flood marked a great discontinuity, both in the course of human history and in the normal operation of the natural processes that God had established supernaturally in the beginning. The rates of most geological processes (such as erosion, sedimentation, tectonism, and volcanism) were vastly accelerated during the year of the flood. God finally allowed the flood to run its course, after which all these rates gradually slowed, though much "residual catastrophism" persists even to the present day.

Job also refers to this drying-up period. "As the waters fail from the sea, and the flood decayeth and drieth up: So man lieth down, and riseth not: till the heavens be no more, they shall not awake, nor be raised out of their sleep" (Job 14:11–12). The language reflects God's post-flood promise to Noah: "While the earth remaineth" (Gen. 8:22), such a flood would never come again, and the basic constants of nature (earth's axial rotation and orbital revolution, which control all daily and seasonal changes) would continue to be uniform until the day of the resurrection at the end of the age.

The dependability of nature and God's promise not to allow another global flood are the subjects of other Joban passages. For example: "He hath compassed the waters with bounds, until the day and night come to an end" (Job 26:10). This passage again reflects God's promise that "day and night shall not cease" and "neither shall there any more be a flood to destroy the earth" (Gen. 8:22; 9:11). God also reminded Job of the flood in these words: "Who shut up the sea with doors, when it brake forth, as if it had issued out of the womb? When I made the cloud the garment thereof, and thick darkness a swaddlingband for it, and brake up for it my decreed place, and set bars and doors, And said, Hitherto shalt thou come, but no further: and here shall thy proud waves be stayed?" (Job 38:8–11). This passage evidently refers to the waters that gushed up out of the subterranean depths on the fearful day that began the great flood, when "the same day were all the fountains of the great deep broken up (Gen. 7:11).

There are even hints of the post-flood Ice Age scattered throughout the Book of Job. When the thermal water vapor blanket (the waters above the firmament) rained on the

earth during the flood, the greenhouse environment dissipated. Snow began to fall in the polar latitudes and eventually great ice sheets fanned out over the northern regions of
Europe, Asia, and North America. This glacial period did not
last for a million years or more, as evolutionary geologists
believe, but it could have persisted for several centuries.

The ice sheets did not extend into Bible lands, but they did
undoubtedly affect their climates, producing much more
rain, snow, and ice than occur today in those regions, known
today for their heat and aridity.

Consequently, it may be significant that there are more
references to cold, snow, ice, and frost in Job than in any
other book of the Bible. It is possible that Job and his friends
had heard tales of the glacial sheets bounding the northern
lands, even though they had not seen them.

In any case, some of the snow references in Job may be
worth noting. For example: "Out of the south cometh the
whirlwind: and cold out of the north. By the breath of God
frost is given: and the breadth of the waters is straightened"
(Job 37:9–10).

The direct words of God, in his final message to Job, are
especially interesting, though still enigmatic. "Hast thou
entered into the treasures of the snow? or hast thou seen the
treasures of the hail, Which I have reserved against the time
of trouble, against the day of battle and war?" (Job
38:22–23). Then in Job 38:29–30, there is perhaps an even
more significant comment, at least with respect to Job's
awareness of the northern ice-covered lakes and seas. "Out
of whose womb came the ice? and the hoary frost of heaven,
who hath gendered it? The waters are hid as with a stone,
and the face of the deep is frozen." The picture of ice emerging as from a womb seems most applicable to the slow
advance of glaciers.

It is possible to interpret all these passages in other ways.
Nevertheless, it seems highly significant that the entire
Book of Job can be so easily and naturally understood in the
context of a world only recently recovered from the devasta-
tion of the great flood.

Ham → Cush → Nimrod

The Worldwide Dispersion

Another world-changing event of the primeval ages was the confusion of languages at Babel and the following dispersion of the nations. This event, described in Genesis 10 and 11, is also reflected in Job.

When Noah and his sons left the ark after the flood God told them: "Be fruitful, and multiply, and replenish [that is, fill] the earth" (Gen. 9:1). Their descendants, however (perhaps excluding Shem and some of his sons), chose instead to remain at Babel under the leadership of Nimrod, son of Cush (same as Ethiopia), son of Ham (Gen. 10:8–10). To thwart this growing rebellion and to enforce his command to fill the earth, God "did there confound the language of all the earth: and from thence did the LORD scatter them abroad upon the face of all the earth" (Gen. 11:9).

This traumatic beginning of the nations seems to be in view in the latter part of Job 12, after Job mentions the flood in verses 14–16. Beginning at verse 17: "He leadeth counsellors away spoiled [possibly a reference to the consultation of Nimrod's rebels 'one to another' planning the insurrection against God 'which they have imagined to do'—note Genesis 11:3–6], and maketh the judges fools," babbling incoherently to each other! "He removeth away the speech of the trusty, and taketh away the understanding of the aged. He poureth contempt upon princes, and weakeneth the strength of the mighty. He discovereth deep things out of darkness, and bringeth out to light the shadow of death" (Job 12:20–22). This may refer to the Satanic conspiracy that persuaded Nimrod to build his tower unto the heavens and to emblaze on its summit astrological signs for worshiping the host of heaven, the rebellious angels under Satan.

Next came the scattering of the various families from Babel, forcing each to find its own geographical region and to establish its own culture. Some succeeded, others died out. "He increaseth the nations, and destroyeth them: he enlargeth the nations, and straiteneth them again. He taketh away the heart of the chief of the people of the earth, and causeth them to wander in a wilderness where there is no way. They grope in the dark without light, and he maketh them to stagger like a drunken man" (Job 12:23–25).

It is worth noting that a number of the tribal names mentioned in Job are first encountered in the Table of Nations (Gen. 10), which listed seventy nations that evidently resulted from the Babel dispersion. Note the following list:

Uz (Gen. 10:23; see Job 1:1);

Sheba (Gen. 10:7, 28; see Job 6:19);

Ophir (Gen. 10:29; see Job 28:16);

Ethiopia (same as Cush, Gen. 10:6; see Job 28:19);

Seba (same as Sabaeans, Gen. 10:7; see Job 1:15).

This comparison further emphasizes the antiquity of Job. The Chaldeans (see Job 1:17) are first mentioned in connection with Abraham's boyhood home in Ur (Gen. 11:28), but Ur may originally have been Uruk, or Erech (Gen. 10:10).

Other tribal names in Job may include Tema, son of Ishmael (Gen. 25:15; see Job 6:19), Teman, grandson of Esau (Gen. 36:15; see Job 2:11); Shuah (son of Abraham by Keturah, as listed in Gen. 25:2, and probable ancestor of Bildad, the Shuhite: see Job 2:11); and Buz (nephew of Abraham, noted in Gen. 22:21, an ancestor of Elihu, as suggested in Job 32:2). All of these long predate Moses.

In addition to the tribes and nations named in the early chapters of Genesis and those known from ancient secular history, many, for some reason (perhaps lack of ability or industry, degenerate habits, or disease), could not compete successfully and eventually died out. These most likely included "cave men" and others now identified only by fragmentary fossils and crude artifacts and often mistakenly classed as evolving hominids or "ape-men."

Job and his contemporaries evidently were aware of some of these degenerate peoples, still barely surviving. Those he noted as wanderers in the wilderness or as those groping in the dark without light (Job 12:24–25) were very likely those living in deserts, jungles, or caves.

Note also his description of certain other brutish people: "For want and famine they were solitary; fleeing into the wilderness in former time desolate and waste, Who cut up mallows by the bushes, and juniper roots for their meat. They were driven forth from among men, (they cried after them as after a thief;) To dwell in the cliffs of the valleys, in caves of the earth, and in the rocks. Among the bushes they brayed; under the nettles they were gathered together. They were children of fools, yea, children of base men: they were viler than the earth" (Job 30:3–8).

Numerous indications scattered through the Book of Job indicate its great antiquity. Its whole outlook and atmosphere is essentially the same as in the early chapters of Genesis. Job probably lived sometime between Abraham and Moses, but he represents a point of view outside that of the genealogical line leading from Abraham to Moses.

God chose Abraham, Isaac, and Jacob for very good reasons, but he had not forgotten his other "sheep . . . which are not of this fold" (John 10:16). In fact, of all the people in the earth in that day, including those in the line of the chosen people, God himself testified that there was no one in all the world giving a better testimony "unto the principalities and powers in heavenly places" (Eph. 3:10) of God's redemptive grace and righteousness than his servant Job.

3

Modern Scientific Insights in Job

In what is probably the oldest book in the Bible, it is remarkable that there are so many references to discoveries or problems of modern science. In addition to the many historical references to creation and the flood, the discourses in the Book of Job contain many allusions to the systems and processes of nature, which people today study in formal scientific disciplines. These references are modern in perspective, with never a hint of the mythical exaggerations and errors characteristic of other ancient writings. Fifteen or more facts of science are suggested in Job that scientists did not discover until recent centuries. A number of other such anticipations of modern science are scattered through the Bible, but Job probably contains more than any other one book.

15 facts

This indicates either the divine inspiration of the Book of

Job or the remarkably up-to-date scientific knowledge of those ancient nations and tribes.

Idolatrous nature-worshiping occultism introduced at Babel subsequently spread around the world as a result of the confusion-of-tongues judgment. This anti-God system—actually an early form of the evolutionary pantheism which still dominates the intellectual and religious establishments of the world—had soon all but eradicated worship of the true Creator and also much of his primeval revelation of the nature and purpose of creation. At the time of Job, however, much of this common heritage was still retained, especially by certain tribes descended from Noah through Shem.

Thus, even though not everything in the discourses of Job and his friends can be considered divinely inspired (God himself, in Job 42:7, testified that much of what they had said was wrong), they nevertheless contain much that is true—scientific truth as well as moral and spiritual truth. The following sections summarize some of the scientific insights.

The Science of Water

Hydrology, the study of water, deals with the occurrence and behavior of water in its natural state. Air and water have been the two necessities for maintaining life ever since the global atmosphere and hydrosphere were established by God on the second day of creation week. The "hydrologic cycle" describes the cooperation of atmosphere and hydrosphere in maintaining a fresh supply of water for the daily needs of all forms of life. Because of its importance, water has been of paramount concern to every tribe and nation since the beginning, and the remains of ancient canals, irrigation systems, reservoirs, and drainage networks are evidence of this truth.

Despite this concern, the concept of the hydrological cycle and its successive phases (evaporation, atmospheric circulation, condensation, precipitation, run-off) was not discovered (or possibly rediscovered) until recent centuries. Yet there are several significant references in Job that are remarkably consistent with modern hydrology and meteorology.

For example, consider Job 28:24–27: "For [God] looketh to the ends of the earth, and seeth under the whole heaven; To make the weight for the winds; and he weigheth the waters by measure. When he made a decree for the rain, and a way for the lightning of the thunder: Then did he see it, and declare it; he prepared it, yea, and searched it out."

We now know that the global weights of air and water must be in critical relationship to each other, and to the earth as a whole, to maintain life on earth. No other planet in the solar system has a significant amount of either air or water, and no other planets are known to exist in the universe. Planet earth is uniquely designed for life, and its atmosphere and hydrosphere are the most important components of that design. If the weights of either air or water were much different than they are, life as we know it could not survive.

This passage is also significant in recognizing that air and wind have weight, a fact not obvious to the physical senses and not confirmed scientifically until about 300 years ago. The study of air flows and their relation to the weight of the air has been developed into the science of aerodynamics, eventually becoming the basis of all modern aerospace developments. The parallel study of water flows and forces is called hydrodynamics, the basis of ship design, hydroelectric plants, and a multitude of other hydraulic systems.

The indication in this Joban passage that there is a parallel between the behavior of air and water was recognized in the late nineteenth century when the sciences of aerodynamics and hydrodynamics were combined into the discipline of fluid dynamics. This key science embraces the behavior of all fluids, including the phenomena of petroleum and natural gas reservoirs and their uses.

The verses cited above may suggest all these future developments, but originally they applied specifically to the hydrologic cycle. The "weight of the winds" controls the worldwide air mass movements that transport the waters evaporated from the oceans inland over the continents. There the waters, also carefully measured by God, fall to the ground to water the earth.

But how is all this accomplished? Water weighs much more than air, so how is it retained in the sky at all? Here is how. "He maketh small the drops of water: they pour down rain according to the vapour thereof: Which the clouds do drop and distil upon man abundantly" (Job 36:27–28).

Water is converted by solar energy into the vapor state. Since water vapor is lighter than air, the winds can first elevate, then transport the water from the oceans to the lands where it is needed. There, under the right conditions, the vapor can condense around dust particles, salt particles, or other nuclei of condensation.

When this happens, clouds are formed. Water vapor is invisible, whereas clouds are aggregations of liquid water droplets. But then the question again must be raised: how do the clouds stay aloft? Job rightly stressed the remarkable nature of this phenomenon. "Dost thou know the balancing of the clouds?" (Job 37:16). They did *not* know in his day. "He bindeth up the waters in his thick clouds; and the cloud is not rent under them" (Job 26:8).

The secret, however, is again in "the weight of the winds" and in the fact that "He maketh small the drops of water." The water droplets are indeed very small, and their weight is sustained by the drag force of the uprushing winds, as the air is pushed skyward due to temperature decrease with elevation.

How is this "balancing of the clouds" finally overcome, so that they can "pour down rain according to the vapour thereof?" The answer is given in Job 37:11. "By watering he wearieth the thick cloud." That is, the water droplets coalesce to form larger and larger drops, which finally become so large that their weight is greater than the drag forces of the uprushing atmospheric turbulence, causing them to fall to the ground as rain or snow.

But then, what makes the small droplets become large enough to do this? Some clouds never fall, while others grow dark and heavy. What makes the difference? The answer is in our original passage. "He made a decree for the rain, and a way for the lightning of the thunder." With the right combination of air turbulence and clouds, the complex forces generate an electrical field that produces lightning discharges. These violent electrical currents, in some complex energy exchange not yet fully understood, cause the small water droplets to bind together with others to form larger drops. Finally, this remarkable series of events delivers the rain to the thirsty ground.

This is also the theme of some of God's rhetorical questions in his challenge to Job and his friends: "Who hath divided a watercourse for the overflowing of waters, or a way for the lightning of thunder; To cause it to rain on the earth, where no man is; on the wilderness, wherein there is no man; To satisfy the desolate and waste ground; and to cause the bud of the tender herb to spring forth? Hath the rain a father: or who hath begotten the drops of dew?" (Job 38:25–28).

After the great flood, the whole world was a wilderness, and there were no men to irrigate or till the ground. In the pre-flood world, there had been no rain (Gen 2:5), but the ground had been watered by a daily mist, or dew, and by a system of rivers fed by artesian springs emerging from the "great deep," a vast system of underground pressurized reservoirs. The antediluvian "waters above the firmament" and the "great deep" had been dissipated at the flood, so God had to devise a new system for watering the earth. This he accomplished by activating the marvelous engine which we know today as the hydrologic cycle.

The Science of Earth

The disciplines of science we call geology and geophysics are also treated in Job. The most basic fact of these sciences is the earth itself—its nature and structure.

A key verse is Job 26:7: "He stretcheth out the north over the empty place, and hangeth the earth upon nothing." The word for empty place (Hebrew *tohu*) is the same word translated "without form" in Genesis 1:2, referring to the formless condition of the original matter of the earth ("dust of the earth") when God first called into existence the space/time/mass universe (Gen. 1:1).

Thus, Job was saying that the north-pointing axis of the earth extended indefinitely beyond the boundaries of earth's surface, pointing to the polar star and orienting both the geography of the earth and the corresponding starscape of the stellar heavens. The "empty space" is not really empty, of course, being occupied by interstellar dust and a variety of particles and radiations. It is, however, "without form," just as the primeval earth had been before the spirit of God moved over it, giving it form by activating the energy of gravitation and energizing it with God's own light.

Furthermore, the earth was not resting on the shoulders of Atlas or on the back of a cosmic elephant. God "hangeth the earth upon nothing." Suspended in the formless void of space without support, the earth is rigidly maintained in its orbit by a mysterious force we call gravity, but which could just as rationally be called nothing—or perhaps better, the will of God.

Job suggests not only that the earth was suspended in space but also that it rotates about its north-projecting axis. "Hast thou commanded the morning since thy days; and caused the dayspring to know his place; That it might take hold of the ends of the earth; that the wicked might be shaken out of it? It is turned as clay to the seal; and they stand as a garment" (Job 38:12–14). Though figurative language, this reflects a true physical process. God is pictured as taking hold of the two ends of the earth's axis and turning it as if it were a clay cylinder receiving an impression from a seal. The seal toward which the earth is turned, however, is not a metallic pattern. Rather, it is the "dayspring," evidently the sun fixed in its place. The welcome light of the morning dispels the formlessness of the earth's surface when shrouded in darkness and unveils the beauties of the earth's structure and verdure. The darkness also hides the wickedness of the earth's inhabitants, but they and their works stand out like a garment exposed to the light of day.

The processes that determine the topography of the earth's surface are studied in the science of geomorphology. The most important of these involves the effects of water in its work of eroding, transporting, and depositing sediments. This process is beautifully summarized in Job 14:18–19: "And surely the mountain falling cometh to nought, and the rock is removed out of his place. The waters wear the stones: thou washest away the things which grow out of the dust of the earth; and thou destroyest the hope of man." The "things" that grow out of the "dust of the earth" may include not only the plants but also the great variety of minerals that crystallize out of the basic elements and which are then cemented together in different types of rocks. These disintegrate through weathering and are carried away by water erosion. Finally even the mountains break up, and their fragments wash away. "He putteth forth his hand upon the rock; he overturneth the mountains by the roots. He cutteth out rivers among the rocks; and his eye seeth every precious thing" (Job 28:9–10).

The process of establishing a post-flood drainage system exposed the "precious things" in the rocks, the beautiful and valuable metals and minerals so highly prized and widely used by man. Chapter 28 of Job mentions a number of these—the "gold of Ophir, with the precious onyx, or the sapphire" (v. 16), the "silver" and the "crystal" (vv. 15–17), "rubies" and the "topaz of Ethiopia" (vv. 18–19). Even the coral and pearl from the sea are mentioned (v. 18). But all these "precious things" are said to be far less valuable than true wisdom and understanding (true science, one might say), which is discovered only through the fear of the Lord.

The land of Uz probably had no seacoast, so Job may never have seen an ocean. Nevertheless, his book includes numerous references to this important feature of the earth's topography. One of the most significant is in God's question: "Hast thou entered into the springs of the sea? or hast thou walked in the search of the depth?" (Job 38:16). Although many of the ancients were accomplished navigators, we assume they had no way of exploring the beds of the deep ocean, as we do today. The many fresh-water springs on the ocean floor and the distinct channels and pathways in the ocean's depths have been a surprising discovery of modern oceanography. Yet God mentioned these facts in his message to Job four thousand years ago.

The waters of the oceans now contain the waters of the great flood, which once were in "the waters above the firmament" and "the great deep" below the antediluvian crust. After these waters "stood above the mountains" (Ps. 104:6), tremendous crustal movements elevated great mountain ranges and opened up great ocean basins into which the flood waters drained (Ps. 104:8). God promised the flood would never return to cover the earth again, and this promise is mentioned three times in Job (26:10; 28:11; 38:8–11). The significance of this promise is obvious when we realize how fragile and tenuous the earth's land/water relations really are. It would take only a minor uplift of the ocean bottoms to send waters over most of the earth's land surfaces. Yet God has promised otherwise, and he has kept that promise. Especially significant is Job 26:10. "He hath compassed the waters with bounds, until the day and night come to an end." The word *compassed* (Hebrew *khug*) means to be made spherical, referring to the shape of the earth, especially to its sea level, the basic datum for earth's geometry. See also Proverbs 8:27 and Isaiah 40:22, where the same word is used, and with the same connotation.

The Stars of the Heavens

The study of the stars has always fascinated mankind. The Book of Job likewise reflects this interest. Bible skeptics often claim that the biblical cosmos pictures a solid vault at the top of the sky, with the stars affixed to this surface. This is not the picture in Job, however (or anywhere else in the Bible, for that matter). Modern astronomy views the extent of the heavens as unlimited, and this is also the indication in Job. "Canst thou by searching find out God? canst thou find out the Almighty unto perfection? It is as high as heaven; what canst thou do?" (Job 11:7–8).

In this simile, the height of heaven is compared to the infinitude of God. This implies that the heavens are unbounded, exactly as modern astronomy indicates. Note also the exclamation of Job 22:12: "Is not God in the height of heaven? and behold the height of the stars, how high they are!"

There is a possible reference to the expanding universe concept of twentieth-century astrophysics in Job 9:8, which says that God "spreadeth out the heavens." Another possible—though questionable—anticipation of astrophysics is the reference in Job 38:7 to "the morning stars" singing together at the foundation of the earth. This verse more likely refers to angels, but perhaps also hints of modern radio astronomy, which uses radio telescopes to measure sonic signals from distant galaxies instead of optical telescopes recording starlight.

More significant is the stress on the dependability and uniformity of stellar positions and movements. "Knowest thou the ordinances of heaven? canst thou set the dominion thereof in the earth?" (Job 38:33). Evolutionists have developed various theories of stellar evolution, but these stars and star systems are not changing at all. As long as men have been observing the stars, their relative positions and motions have not changed. They are used to set the time, to determine latitude and longitude, to establish directions and locations anywhere on earth for navigation and other uses that require extreme precision. They were, in fact, created to "be for signs, and for seasons, and for days, and years" (Gen. 1:14).

The year after year reliability of the heavens is best seen by the annual progression of the heavenly constellations, marking the regular advance of the seasons. "Canst thou bring forth Mazzaroth in his season?" (Job 38:32). *Mazzaroth* refers specifically to the monthly signs of the Zodiac, which have been essentially the same in every nation since the beginning of history.

Not only are the individual stars dependable, but so are the groupings known as constellations. Even though the stars in each constellation usually have no connection with each other in the heavens, they are so positioned that they seem, to people viewing them from the earth, to be related to one another. Thus they have always been so identified. These constellations and their traditional names are still used by modern astronomers, even though these astronomers decry what they consider to be their astrological and mythological origin.

As a matter of fact, in Job, God himself is identified as the author of the constellations and of individual stars. Several are named. "[God] maketh Arcturus, Orion, and Pleiades, and the chambers of the south" (Job 9:9). "By his Spirit he hath garnished the heavens; his hand hath formed the crooked serpent" (Job 26:13). In his own discourse, God issued the challenge: "Canst thou bind the sweet influences of Pleiades, or loose the bands of Orion? Canst thou bring forth Mazzaroth [i.e., the Zodiac constellations] in his season? or canst thou guide Arcturus with his sons? Knowest thou the ordinances of heaven? canst thou set the dominion thereof in the earth?" (Job 38:31–33).

None of the constellations named are the twelve major signs of the Zodiac, but all are related in some way to one or another of these signs. We can conclude that this is what God meant when he said the stars were to be used for "signs" as well as for "seasons" (Gen. 1:14). Since God does nothing without a holy purpose, we can be sure that these sidereal signs were *not* to be used as astrological signs. God's Word, in fact, forbids the practice of astrology (e.g.,

Isa. 47:12–14), which has long been associated with evolutionary pantheism and occultism.

In some way, therefore, these constellations must have symbolized to the ancient patriarchs God's purposes in creation and his promises of a coming Redeemer. This primeval message has been corrupted Satanically into the fantasy messages of the astrologers, but, since we now have God's written Word, it is no longer needed. To the early generations, however, it may have served as a memory device, perpetually calling to mind the primeval promises given to Adam, Enoch, and Noah, and those in the line of chosen patriarchs. Even when the world was destroyed in the great flood, the starry heavens remained the same, conveying God's promises to future generations, at least until enough of the written Word was available to make the sidereal signs no longer necessary.

It may be impossible at this late date to fully recover this ancient "gospel in the stars," though a number of attempts have been made.[1] For that matter, since we no longer *need* this revelation, its main value now is as a weapon in our arsenal of Christian evidences.

In any case, "the heavens declare the glory of God" (Ps. 19:1), and the Lord Jesus Christ is "the brightness of his glory" (Heb. 1:3). "For God, who commanded the light to shine out of darkness, hath shined in our hearts, to give the light of the knowledge of the glory of God in the face of Jesus Christ" (2 Cor. 4:6).

It is significant that this oldest book of the Bible contains more specific references to the constellations than any other book, suggesting that God-fearing men of that age were very much aware of the divine significance of these God-ordained star groups. On the other hand, it is also significant that the Book of Job does not deal specifically with any such message, stressing instead the regulated movements of all the

1. For a brief summary of these studies, see Henry M. Morris, *The Biblical Basis for Modern Science* (Grand Rapids: Baker Book House, 1984), 176–184, 476.

stars through the heavens, as a testimony of the wisdom and power of their Creator. That message is the same today, and more needed than ever, in an age when the idea of an omnipotent Creator is rejected and ridiculed.

The Laws of Nature

Throughout Job we also find a strong emphasis on the dependability of the laws and constants now controlling God's completed creation. Unlike other ancient books, Job has no hints of magical acts or any other occult practices. There are not any divine miracles recorded (except for Job's eventual healing, if that is considered miraculous), although both Job and Elihu mentioned their faith in the future resurrection of the body (Job 19:26; 33:28). This is especially surprising in view of the many miracles recorded in the Mosaic writings of the Pentateuch. Job records one demonic visitation, as well as God's personal revelation (Job 4:12–21; 38:1–42:8), but throughout the book there is repeated emphasis on the reliability of God's providential—rather than miraculous—control of his creation.

This regularity in nature is the fundamental premise of modern science. Furthermore, God revealed to Job that the same laws apply throughout the universe—not just on earth. This is one major implication of his challenge in Job 38:33: "Knowest thou the ordinances of heaven? canst thou set the dominion thereof in the earth?" God's universe is not a multiverse!

The most significant entity with which modern science must deal in the physical universe is that of energy. Everything that exists in the physical universe is energy, in one form or another (e.g., heat, sound, electricity). Even matter is essentially a form of energy. Also, everything that happens is an energy conversion process—one form of energy being converted to another as it accomplishes some function.

The most fundamental form of energy is *light*! In fact, all the electro-magnetic force systems (all types of energy except gravity and the nuclear forces) are essentially different forms of light energy operating at different wave lengths. Even the nuclear forces involve the velocity of light. God's first Word, when he energized the created cosmos, was: "Let there be light!" (Gen. 1:3).

In speaking to Job, God uttered a profoundly modern scientific question when he asked "Where is the way where light dwelleth?" (Job 38:19). That is, light is not to be located in a certain place or situation. Neither does it simply appear, or disappear, instantaneously. Light is traveling! It dwells in a "way," always on the way to someplace else. Though usually traveling in waves, sometimes it seems to move as a stream of particles, but it is always moving.

God also asked: "As for darkness, where is the place thereof?" (Job 38:19). When light stops traveling, there is darkness. Thus, darkness is static, staying in place; but light is dynamic, dwelling in a way. Bound up in these energies of light, the electromagnetic spectrum, and the relation between matter and energy are all the phenomena of the physical cosmos.

God also asked: "By what way is the light parted?" (Job 38:24). This may refer not only to the visible light spectrum (red to violet) but also to all the physical systems developed around the basic entity of light.

A fascinating and quite modern use of energy is suggested in the divine question: "Canst thou send lightnings, that they may go, and say unto thee, Here we are?" (Job 38:35). One of the most important technological achievements of modern science is the development of principles and devices that can transform electrical energy into sound energy and light energy, transmitting messages and even pictures over vast distances by lightning-fast electronic communications.

There may be other hints of future scientific discoveries hidden here in this ancient book, but perhaps of even greater significance is the fact that in a 4000-year-old book filled with numerous references to natural phenomena, there are *no* scientific mistakes or fallacies. Yet the Book of Job was not written as a book of science at all, but as a book dealing with the most basic problems of human life in relation to God and his plans for his people.

4

A Godly Man and
the Scientific Method

As we proceed to the actual narrative and message of the book of Job, it is interesting to note—in a book with so many references to science—that this absorbing drama can be considered as a scientific test by God, conducted in the framework of what people today would call the scientific method.

As commonly defined, the scientific method is the experimental method: a scientific hypothesis proposed by the researcher followed by a test that fails if the hypothesis is wrong. If the hypothesis passes the test, however, this does not necessarily prove it to be true; the test proved only that it worked for the conditions tested. Therefore, a second type of falsification test is proposed and the hypothesis is examined under the second set of conditions. And so on.

If the hypothesis fails any one of the tests, it is considered falsified and must be rejected. Thus an experimental test can *disprove* a hypothesis, but can never completely *prove* it, until it has passed all conceivable tests. After it passes a good number of such tests, it may be called a scientific theory and, eventually, even a scientific law.

This is very similar to the succession of events described in Job. God proposes a hypothesis, as it were, regarding the character and behavior of Job. Satan, the "Adversary," challenges him to a falsification test. Job passes the test, but then Satan proposes a second, more demanding test.

Job also passes the second test, and then we hear nothing more from Satan, at least not directly. We can be sure, however, that he has not given up, and the rest of Job is taken up with his third test, the most severe of all.

Satan in God's Presence

Chapters 1 and 2 of Job are often called its Prologue, with Chapter 42 as its Epilogue. It seems that these beginning and ending chapters may have been written by Moses, in order to set the book in proper context. It is also possible that Job wrote them himself later by direct inspiration. If so, however, he could not have known about the Satanic background of his troubles during the time he was going through them.

That background was, indeed, remarkable. By whatever means the information was received by Moses (or whoever wrote this Prologue), we are given a glimpse of the court of God in heaven, and it is an amazing scene.

"Now there was a day when the sons of God came to present themselves before the LORD, and Satan came also among them" (Job 1:6). The sons of God are the angels (see Job 38:7), and the angels had been created by God to "do his commandments, hearkening unto the voice of his word" (Ps. 103:20). What, then, is Satan doing among them?

The very name of Satan means adversary, and he has been God's great adversary almost since the beginning. Since Job is the oldest book in the Bible, except for the early chapters of Genesis, this is really the first mention of his name. Using the body of the serpent in the Garden of Eden, Satan persuaded Adam and Eve to disobey God's command and not to hearken to the voice of his Word. In the final book of the Bible, he is identified clearly as "that old serpent, called the Devil, and Satan, which deceiveth the whole world" (Rev. 12:9).

Satan is not eternal, however, like God, and he was not created as the adversary, or deceiver, but as "the anointed cherub" (Ez. 28:14), evidently the highest of all the angelic hierarchy. God testified to him: "Thou wast perfect in thy ways from the day that thou wast created, till iniquity was found in thee" (Ez. 28:15).

The iniquity found in him was pride—pride so monstrous that he believed he could overthrow God and reign over the creation. "Thine heart was lifted up because of thy beauty, thou hast corrupted thy wisdom by reason of thy brightness" (Ez. 28:17). "For thou hast said in thine heart, I will ascend into heaven, I will exalt my throne above the stars of God: . . . I will be like the most high" (Isa. 14:13–14). Because of this rebellion, God cast him out of heaven.

The passages from which the above excerpts were taken (Ez. 28:12–17 and Isa. 14:12–15) were directed initially to the kings of Tyre and Babylon, so many commentators deny that they apply to Satan. However, most Bible-believing scholars concur in this application, for the good reason that the statements made could not possibly apply in their fullness to any earthly king. These two kings were not just demon-possessed, but Satan-possessed, so God spoke in the same address to the human king and to the malignant spirit controlling him.

There are other references to Satan's fall in the Bible and numerous references to his current activities. The latter are all designed to defeat God's purposes in creation, especially his purposes for the men and women created in his image.

His ongoing desire to usurp the place of God was shown when he tempted Christ. Knowing that Jesus was the Word made flesh, the eternal Creator incarnate, Satan sought earnestly to get Jesus to worship him (Matt. 4:8–10), apparently convinced that this would give him preeminence over God. He failed, of course, but his effort shows that his initial fall did not deter him in his quest for God's throne. He will battle God to the very end (Rev. 20:7–10), still thinking he can win.

He had been created "full of wisdom" (Ez. 28:12), and he surely knows the Scriptures (he even quoted one to Jesus— Matt. 4:6), so the apparent reason for his age-long rebellion is his refusal to believe God's Word, doubting that God is really the Creator and thus able to fulfill his promises.

This may partially explain the repeated emphasis in the Book of Job on God's creation of all things, including even the primeval space/time/matter universe itself. This must have been the environment in which Satan and all other angels had first come into consciousness, when they were created. Even though they had later observed God create the earth, stars, and living beings, they had not seen him create the universe itself. Thus, Satan may have persuaded himself that God, like the angels, must simply have "evolved" somehow, out of the eternal primordial chaos—or perhaps out of a "quantum fluctuation in a primeval state of nothingness," as modern-day physicists are currently speculating. In any event, he considers himself as fundamentally equal with God, only temporarily held in subjection under him.

It was in some such attitude that he dared to come into God's presence, along with all the holy angels, and to challenge God to a test. Even though Satan had been demoted from his supreme position over the angels, God allowed him a great measure of freedom and power in the world. Even Michael the archangel treats him respectfully (Jude 9), and he is specifically called "the god of this world" by the apostle Paul (2 Cor. 4:4).

Having lost in his attempt to defeat Jesus, Satan's only recourse is to continue trying to destroy God's plans for men and women by getting them to renounce God and join him (usually unwittingly) in his own rebellion. He has been eminently successful in this by developing a variety of pantheistic religious systems, including modern evolutionary humanism and countless other deceptive devices. "Your adversary, the devil, as a roaring lion, walketh about, seeking whom he may devour" (1 Pet. 5:8).

Satan, powerful though he is, is not omnipresent, however. He must "walk about" seeking people who will rebel against God as he did. After such a period of reconnaissance he came to speak to God. "Whence comest thou?" asked God. "From going to and fro in the earth, and from walking up and down in it," replied Satan (Job 1:7). God knew that Satan had planned a great challenge to his authority, so he led him right to the point.

The Conflict of the Ages

"And the LORD said unto Satan, Hast thou considered my servant Job, that there is none like him in the earth, a perfect and an upright man, one that feareth God, and escheweth evil?" (Job 1:8).

God, being omniscient, knew why Satan had come and knew that he was familiar with Job and his testimony. This was a leading question, giving Satan the opportunity to propose his test. What is *not* obvious is why Satan wanted to carry out this particular test, and why God was willing to allow Satan such an opportunity. Herein must lie the key to the purpose and message of the Book of Job.

Since the book does not explicitly reveal this key, we cannot be dogmatic. Nevertheless, we now have what neither Job nor Moses had in their days: the complete written Word of God. And we have enough information revealed in Scripture to get some understanding of this great cosmic drama, Satan's rebellious attempt to defeat God's purposes in creation.

All of these purposes center on that special body of men and women created in God's own image and redeemed from

sin by his work of salvation, who one day will share personal
fellowship with him and serve him throughout eternity.

Angels

Angels, on the other hand, though created before man,
were created to serve as "ministering spirits" to all who
would someday become God's "heirs of salvation" (Heb.
1:14). Although angels had the freedom to disobey God, they
were not created in God's image, as were Adam and Eve.
Neither were they given the ability to multiply (Gen. 1:28), as
were Adam and Eve. Perhaps these limitations contributed
to the willingness of a great host of them to listen to Satan
when he proposed rebellion. Perhaps they saw a chance to
mold the universe for their own benefit rather than serve a
proliferating race of human beings. In fact, they might even
be able to use this remarkable ability of reproduction
(which God had somehow devised for earth's inhabitants) to
serve their own ends.

By possessing the serpent's body and taking advantage of
Eve's innocence, Satan deceived both Eve and Adam into the
sin of unbelief and disobedience. Using the same lie with
which he had deceived himself, he promised, "Ye shall be as
gods" (Gen. 3:5). Actually the word *gods* (Hebrew *Elohim*) is
the same as *God*. So Satan was saying that they were fundamentally no different from their maker. The only difference
was chronological priority—the same evolutionary premise
with which he had deceived himself and the angels who
followed him.

He also corrupted their first son, Cain, and practically the
entire human race by the time of Noah. To do this, he used
the services of many of the "sons of God" who had followed
him in his rebellion. These once-holy angels had at one time
joined with all the other "sons of God" when they "shouted
for joy" at the laying of the foundations of the earth (Job
38:7). Now, however, they "kept not their first estate, but left
their own habitation...going after strange flesh" (Jude
6–7). "The sons of God came in unto the daughters of man,
and they bare children to them, the same became mighty
men which were of old, men of renown" (Gen. 6:4).

equals angels

These "sons of God" (Hebrew *bene elohim*) in Genesis were the same as those mentioned in Job, if language and usage mean anything, especially in Genesis and Job, two books of the same antiquity and authenticity, both probably edited and transmitted by Moses. The term is never used elsewhere in the Old Testament, although a few similar phrases are used (e.g., Ps. 29:1; 89:6; Dan. 3:25), all of which also refer to angels.

It is very doubtful, however, that these rebellious sons of God actually cohabited with human women. It is more likely that they entered and used the bodies of ungodly men, as Satan once used the body of a serpent. As demons, or evil spirits, the fallen angels controlled the bodies of these men to produce offspring that they could control from birth, producing a generation of such monstrous size and wickedness that "all flesh had corrupted his way upon the earth" (Gen. 6:12). God finally had to send the great flood to "destroy them with the earth" (Gen. 6:13).

Satan and his followers had seemingly been very successful in their strategy, but they had failed to reach one key man. "Noah found grace in the eyes of the Lord" (Gen. 6:8). Noah and his family were preserved in the ark and, after the flood, "of them was the whole earth overspread (Gen. 9:19).

On the other hand, "God spared not the angels that sinned, but cast them down to hell, and delivered them into chains of darkness, to be reserved unto judgment" (2 Peter 2:4). Except for the multitude of men and women whose souls had been captured by Satan, his strategy had backfired, and many of his angels were of no more use to him.

He was not about to concede defeat, however. His strategy at Babel, using King Nimrod, was different. With only a small population this time, he worked primarily through one man—evidently a very powerful and popular leader. Again he was successful in instigating a unified rebellion against God.

This effort was thwarted by the confusion of tongues and subsequent dispersion. Satan henceforth had to work his deceptions in many different nations, cultures, and tongues, making a unified rebellion more difficult. In one important respect, however, his efforts at Babel were successful. Under the guidance of Satan and his hierarchy of "principalities and powers" of darkness in the heavenly places (see Eph. 6:12), Nimrod and his associates had developed a very effective religious system. Worship centered on a great temple at the summit of Babel's tower, probably emblazoned with the signs of the Zodiac, as were many other temple towers of antiquity later patterned after Babel.

The original gospel story had, as noted before, been preserved in all probability by the meanings impressed on these signs, and Nimrod may have used this to persuade people to worship God there. Gradually these evangelical meanings were altered into astrological signs and the "host of heaven" (really the fallen angels, but interpreted as various gods and goddesses personifying the forces and systems of nature) began to be worshipped. Thus began the decline described so graphically in Romans 1:21–32, as summarized by the sad phrase: "They worshiped and served the creature [creation] more than the Creator" (Rom. 1:25).

At the dispersion, the tribes carried this religious system with them as they scattered around the world. Although for a while they all retained some knowledge of the true God of creation, almost all eventually took on one form or another of the Babylonian religion learned under Nimrod. This is why the Bible calls Babylon "the mother of harlots and abominations of the earth" (Rev. 17:5).

Thus, all the non-monotheistic religions of the world, ancient and modern, have developed from the Babylonian system. All have been pantheistic, polytheistic, astrological, animistic, and idolatrous. All are essentially nature religions, all denying the existence of a true Creator God and assuming the eternal existence of the universe as the ultimate reality. All are, therefore, forms of evolutionism, not substantially different from the modern system that falsely professes to represent modern science.

God's Scientific Hypothesis

In spite of these developments, God is actively carrying out his plan of redemption. Every age has had at least a few—like Noah and Job—who continued to believe in the true God and to trust his Word, including his primeval promise of a coming Redeemer.

At the time of Job, which was only a few centuries after the flood and even less after the dispersion, Satan had not yet accomplished this worldwide conversion to evolutionary pantheism. Many of the nations retained much knowledge of God, and had not yet declined into the polytheistic pantheism dominating Egypt, Assyria, and other nations. Even in these monotheistic nations, however, people were developing humanistic attitudes, forgetting God's great purposes in creation, focusing more on themselves and their own immediate comforts, and associating personal affluence with spirituality and God's favor.

In such a context, God called Abraham to leave his comfortable home in Ur of the Chaldees and go out to an unknown land, relying only on God and his Word (Gen. 11:31–12:3; Acts 7:2–5; Heb. 11:8–10). It was also in this context that the great drama of Job was taking place.

If not a contemporary of Abraham, Job lived shortly before or shortly after him. Even though God chose Abraham to carry on the line of promise, he regarded Job as such a paragon of true faith and righteousness that he said: "there is none like him in the earth." Three times, in fact, we are told that Job was "perfect and upright, and one that feared God, and eschewed evil" (Job 1:1, 8; 2:3).

Job was "the greatest of all the men of the east" (Job 1:3), known far and wide for his wisdom and God-honoring righteousness. He believed all of God's Word, in whatever form he knew it, and sought to obey all God's laws—helping the needy, instructing the unlearned, and, in general, doing all that one could ever ask of a believer in the true God in any age (see Job 23:12; 29:11–25). He never claimed to be sinless (Job 7:20–21), and he knew that he could only come to God by a substitutionary sacrifice. As head of the family, he offered sacrifices not only for himself but also for his children (Job 1:5). He believed God's promise to send the Redeemer and believed that through him he would have eternal life (Job 19:25–27).

Satan, from his forays up and down, to and fro, in the earth, was well aware that Job was the most godly man in all the earth and he probably blamed Job more than any other that many nations still followed the true God of creation. Satan had allowed one man, Noah, to escape his control in an earlier assault on God, and this had led to a great loss. It would not do to let Job's influence continue to grow and perhaps thwart Satan's strategy of promoting worldwide pantheism, which, if unhindered, could be transformed into worldwide Satanism. Consequently, Satan knew he must get Job to rebel against God.

But Job was the primary exhibit of the efficacy of God's own program, and he had been specially blessed and protected by God as a result. Satan could no more reach Job with his usual deceptions than he could win Noah, back in the antediluvian age.

In this setting, Satan must have decided to challenge God to let him put Job to a real test. He had been permitted to do this once before with Adam and Eve, and his efforts had been crowned with success. If he could get Job to curse God, the entire plan of redemption could perhaps be dealt a mortal blow. Multitudes of other believers would follow Job into apostasy, and God would be forgotten by the human race. Or so Satan hoped.

The Great Experiment

God, anticipating Satan's challenge, put forth his own "scientific hypothesis," maintaining that his servant Job was perfect and upright, fearing God, eschewing evil, so resolute in his faith that he could never be seduced away from his position. Satan forthwith proposed an experiment, a "falsification test," as it were. "Put forth thine hand now, and touch all that he hath, and he will curse thee to thy face" (Job 1:11).

The Lord had greatly blessed Job with great wealth, a large family, and many servants. Furthermore, Job was greatly admired, his counsel heeded by his whole nation and by other nations around him. God had, as Satan charged, "made an hedge around him, and about his house, and about all that he hath" (Job 1:10). No wonder he was faithful to God! But would he continue to serve God "for nought?" (Job 1:9).

God does not always bless his faithful servants with great prosperity. Think of Paul, for example, and all the martyrs. Why Job, then? The reason seems to be that prosperity was to be a factor in Job's testing. "Known unto God are all his works from the beginning of the world" (Acts 15:18). God, being omniscient, knew that this test must someday be made. In order for the test to be the most severe that could be brought to bear, his loss must be the most severe of all time. Thus, Job first had to be blessed in greatest measure before he could be tried in greatest measure.

God allowed Satan to conduct the test. "Behold, all that he hath is in thy power; only upon himself put not forth thine hand" (Job 1:12).

Then the blow fell. In just one day, Job had all his wealth destroyed, all his servants slain, and his ten children killed in a sudden tornado. Job received the tragic news from different sources within a few minutes of each other (Job 1:13–19).

How many Christians today could endure such a succession of devastating blows without losing their love for the Lord, if not their faith as well. Multitudes have turned their backs on God with far less cause.

Yet Job "fell down upon the ground, and worshipped" (Job 1:20). If it is the Lord who has blessed, then he has the right to withdraw his blessings. We do not merit his goodness, so what right have we to complain when he withholds it?

This was Job's reaction. "The LORD gave, and the LORD hath taken away; blessed be the name of the LORD. In all this, Job sinned not, nor charged God foolishly" (Job 1:21–22).

We learn another significant fact from this account. Satan, as "the prince of the power of the air" and as "the prince of this world" has a significant measure of control over the timing and magnitude of the earth's physical processes (Eph. 2:2; John 12:31). With the great wisdom possessed by the devil and his angels, they are often capable of performing apparent miracles by manipulating physical factors that control process rates and locations and thereby causing them to occur to fit their purposes. Angels cannot perform miracles of creation; only God can create. But Satan could have been responsible for the electrical fire storm that consumed Job's sheep and shepherds and for the tornado that killed his children. Similarly, Satan and his demonic minions have the power to implant such strong impressions in the minds of ungodly men that they will (unconsciously or consciously) do their bidding. Thus, he prevailed upon the marauding Sabeans and Chaldeans to steal the rest of Job's livestock and to slay his remaining servants.

Not all such phenomena are directly caused by Satan. The natural processes of the world entail occasional storms, and holy angels and God himself can control any of the processes that the fallen angels can. We see here, however, that on some occasions these phenomena can have a Satanic cause, if God allows. The same applies to our own reasoning and decision-making processes, so we need to consider all these possibilities prayerfully when difficult circumstances arise in our own lives.

Job had no idea that Satan was behind his own troubles. As far as we can tell, Job knew nothing about Satan at all, though he may have known about the serpent in the garden and, perhaps, the sin of the antediluvian angels. He could only attribute his sudden troubles to the will of God; and though he did not understand it, he maintained his trust in God.

But Satan had not completed his experiment. He returned to God and proposed a second falsification test, more severe than the first. "Skin for skin, yea, all that a man hath will he give for his life. But put forth thine hand now, and touch his bone and his flesh, and he will curse thee to thy face" (Job 2:4–5).

God also permitted this test. "Behold, he is in thine hand; but save his life" (Job 2:6). Acting as quickly as before, Satan infected Job with a painful and loathsome disease. His body was inflamed "with sore boils from the sole of his foot unto his crown" (Job 2:7).

Having been cast out of the city as a pauper and leper, Job had to use fragments of broken pottery from the city's ash heap to scratch himself (Job 2:8). He was so hideous, his friends did not recognize him at first (2:12). He could barely eat (3:24); he was infested with worms (7:5); he had difficulty breathing (9:18); his breath was so malodorous that not even his wife could approach him (19:17); he seemed nothing but skin and bones (19:20); his skin was blackened (30:30); and he ran a continual high fever (30:30). Some say his disease was leprosy, others say elephantiasis, but it is doubtful that anyone had ever had an affliction such as Job's.

To make matters even worse, Job then lost his wife. He did not lose her to the grave, as he did his children. She abandoned him, advising him to "Curse God, and die!" (Job 2:9), which is exactly what Satan hoped he would do. Apparently she had already lost her faith (after all, she too had lost her possessions and her children). But Job merely chided her for being foolish, reminding her of all the good they had received from God. "In all this did not Job sin with his lips" (Job 2:10).

We see here that Satan can inflict human beings with sickness when it suits his purpose and when God allows. The apostle Paul experienced such an assault. "Lest I should be exalted above measure...there was given to me a thorn in the flesh, the messenger of Satan to buffet me" (2 Cor. 12:7).

Again, physical illness or infirmity is not necessarily an attack of Satan. This may be the explanation, and should be considered when the circumstances indicate, but in every case there are many other reasons that must also be examined. Furthermore, Satanic and demonic powers can also *heal* when it suits their purposes, at least in certain situations. Note the many healings reputedly achieved in occultic religions, for example.

The fundamental illness is the aging process, which culminates in death and afflicts all people. The basic reason for universal death is universal sin, which also afflicts all people.

Job's incomparable illness was caused by Satan, but Job could not know this; he could only attribute it to the will of God. Though his suffering was nearly unbearable, Job retained his faith and his moral and spiritual integrity.

Satan does not return to heaven to acknowledge his defeat, however. The test is still far from over. It is one thing to endure poverty, loneliness, and pain for a few days, but it is altogether another thing to have them drag on and on, with no relief or hope in sight. Job's afflictions would continue for many months (Job 29:2), and his faith would be tested to the very breaking point.

5

Miserable Comforters

As testimony to Job's wide influence, the news of his sudden calamities carried into other countries. From three different regions came friends to see for themselves what had happened, "to mourn with him and to comfort him" (Job 7:11). These were Eliphaz the Temanite, Bildad the Shuhite, and Zophar the Naamathite, each evidently a cultured and prosperous leader among his own people. All had known Job in better days, possibly holding positions comparable to Job's in their own communities.

The narrative does not say how long it took them to arrive. The news had to reach them, and then they had to make arrangements for a long absence from their home responsibilities, followed by the journey itself. By the time they reached Job, they were appalled at what they saw. His appearance was so hideous that they could not even recognize him at first. His local acquaintances, and perhaps even his wife, had abandoned him to his misery, and Job sat alone on the city's ash dump. Overcome with grief, Job's friends could not even speak.

They sat near Job and shared his mourning in silence for a full seven days and nights, not knowing what to say. They had intended to comfort him, but when they realized his appalling situation, they could think of no words of hope or encouragement. They could think of only one explanation for such a calamity: it must be a judgment from God. Although Job had been exemplary in character and behavior all his life, there seemed to be no other explanation.

Evidently Elihu, the Buzite, also arrived sometime during the first week, though he is not mentioned at this point. He is not identified as one of Job's friends, perhaps because he was much younger than the other three. Nevertheless, he had heard the news and was so curious about the spiritual meaning of such an amazing event that he came to find out for himself.

The Eliphaz Solution

Finally the silence was broken, as was Job himself. He had patiently endured, probably for many long months, a tremendous weight of loss and suffering. The discourses that follow evidently took place all in one day, the day that climaxed and finally brought an end to all his sufferings.

He had suffered months of agony and bereavement with no loss of faith. "Shall we receive good at the hand of God, and shall we not receive evil?" were his own words of comfort to his complaining wife (Job 2:10). But when his three respected friends came to comfort him, and yet could find nothing at all to say for an entire week, it finally became more than he could bear. He suddenly poured out words of anguish in a great and effusive torrent, all expressing his wish to die rather than go on suffering.

Many other suffering saints have expressed the same desire, but none more eloquently than Job. He even "cursed his day" (Job 3:1)—that is, the day he was born—apparently forgetting for the moment, as his wife had, all the good days they had enjoyed. Even in this lapse, however, he refused to "curse God and die," as his wife had urged (Job 2:9) or to "curse thee to thy face," as Satan had predicted (Job 2:5).

Job revealed that even in the days of his prosperity he had feared that the good days could not last indefinitely. "For the thing which I greatly feared is come upon me, and that which I was afraid of is come unto me" (Job 3:25). Even though he knew he had lived a godly life, he realized his blessings were undeserved and that God could withdraw them someday. As he would say later: "Man that is born of a woman is of few days, and full of trouble" (Job 14:1). This is a beneficial truth for every believer to remember. The blessings we enjoy are always gifts of God's grace, not comforts we have earned, and we need to prepare ourselves spiritually for the days of testing that will surely come.

Job's outburst finally gave Eliphaz the Temanite the opening he had wanted. Sadly, however, instead of trying to comfort and encourage his friend, he spoke sharp words of rebuke and discouragement. This set the tone for the subsequent counsel from Bildad and Zophar as well. The three friends had evidently consulted together on the matter before they came to Job, for in concluding his first message, Eliphaz said: "Lo this, we have searched it, so it is; hear it, and know thou it for thy good" (Job 5:27). They must have decided together what they should tell Job, with Eliphaz being chief spokesman for the three. There is no indication that they had prayed for Job or about what to say.

The reason Eliphaz was elected spokesman, and the main reason for their confidence, was evidently a remarkable visitation Eliphaz had experienced before setting out on his journey to counsel Job:

> Now a thing was secretly brought to me, and mine ear received a little thereof. In thoughts from the visions of the night, when deep sleep falleth on men, fear came upon me, and trembling, which made all my bones to shake. Then a spirit passed before my face; the hair of my flesh stood up: It

not God's Holy Spirit

stood still, but I could not discern the form thereof: an image
was before mine eyes, there was silence, and I heard a voice,
saying...(Job 4:12–16).

Not from God

This mysterious spirit was not God's Holy Spirit speaking
words of divine inspiration. God later rebuked all the counsel of Eliphaz and his friends, which was largely based on
the revelation received from this spirit. For the same reason,
it was not one of God's holy angels either. Although angels
appeared to men on occasion during biblical days, their
appearances and messages were never like this.

We conclude therefore, that this was an evil spirit, speaking words of apparent piety and partial truth. In reality,
however, they were deceptive and misleading words, for this
is how Satan works. He can appear as "an angel of light" and
his angelic servants as "ministers of righteousness" (2 Cor.
11:14–15). Perhaps this night visitor was Satan himself, in
view of the importance of the mission, or at least one of his
"principalities and powers," not a run-of-the mill demon;
the latter seem to be more useful in terrifying than in de-
ceiving.

But why would he come to Eliphaz at this time? The
reason must be connected somehow with the pending visit
of Eliphaz to Job. Satan, knowing that Eliphaz was Job's
respected friend and counselor, may have decided this was
the best way to get to Job and to cause him to lose his faith
and renounce the Lord.

The cosmic scientific test was evidently still in progress!
Satan had not acknowledged defeat, and God, with all his
heavenly host, observed carefully from the heavens the ongoing experiment, but in accord with the terms of the test,
they did not interfere. Satan could do his best to destroy
Job's faith, and God would not even allow Job to die. The
thought of suicide evidently never crossed Job's mind, as he
continued to trust God, knowing that his life had been God's
gift. Job was entirely on his own, except for his three
friends, and the devil had deceived them into trying to press
Job beyond the limits even of *his* great faith. Furthermore,

they would do this work of Satan while thinking they were speaking for God.

This was a diabolically clever scheme, and it almost worked. Eliphaz led Bildad and Zophar into the same line of thinking. Then, as a back-up, in case these three could not bring Job to defeat, Satan had one more weapon in reserve—the pious young Elihu, also prepared by a special demonic revelation to attack Job's spiritual integrity.

Demonic Deception

Became Bitter or Better due to circumstance

Part of Satan's strategy with Eliphaz was to include much truth in his message, but it became a lie when the *essential* truth was omitted.

> Shall mortal man be more just than God? shall a man be more pure than his maker? Behold, he put no trust in his servants; and his angels he charged with folly: How much less in them that dwell in houses of clay, whose foundation is in the dust, which are crushed before the moth? They are destroyed from morning to evening: they perish for ever without any regarding it. Doth not their excellency which is in them go away? they die, even without wisdom (Job 4:17–21).

partially true but omit God's grace & love.

These words are true enough, as far as they go, but their message is false because they ignore the all-important dimension of grace and love in the heart of God. These bitter words exactly reflect what must be Satan's perspective on man's creation. Having rejected God's purpose for their own creation—that of serving as God's ministers to the heirs of salvation (Heb. 1:14)—Satan and his angels hate God and despise man. To them, men and women are nothing but perishing houses of clay, on their way back to the dust.

Note also the absence of any reference to sin in this spiritual diatribe. The spirit recalls bitterly how God charged his angels with folly, but he does not call it by its true name: sin or rebellion against their Creator. He does not even acknowledge that the sin that brought about the condition of man so ridiculed by this wicked spirit was guided by Satan.

Nowhere in his revelation to Job's friend is there any mention of the glorious truth that God had created men and woman in his own image. And there is no reference to God's promise of a coming Redeemer who would destroy Satan and all his works (Gen. 3:15). Nor does he mention that God, in the meantime, had instituted substitutionary animal sacrifice as a means of temporary atonement for those who would return to God in repentance and faith.

This spirit's message was one of cynicism and despair. The spirit cunningly left Eliphaz to draw his own conclusions.

With no recognition of God's mercy or gracious promise of salvation in a message supposedly sent by the Lord, the only conclusion Eliphaz could draw was that such a holy God must punish evil and bless goodness, in an inevitable cause-and-effect relationship built into the very nature of things. Humans eventually die, so temporal earthly benefits must be the only indication that a person is in harmony with the holiness of God. Conversely, unusual deprivation or suffering must mean that the person had fallen out of favor with God.

This demonic perversion of divine omnipotence and human impotence soon infected the thinking, and therefore the counsel, of Job's three friends as they tried to understand his situation. They were all still theistic creationists, not yet humanistic pantheists like those in most of the nations around them were becoming. They did have some knowledge of God's laws and, perhaps, a faint understanding of his primeval promises, but all this was now further corrupted by this ostensible revelation of human hopelessness received by Eliphaz.

Since they themselves were prosperous and respected, Job's friends could not bring themselves to acknowledge that his sufferings might be unrelated to sins. To do so would mean that they too were vulnerable to disaster. If moral uprightness and belief in God were not sufficient to assure God's blessings, trials like Job's might strike them someday as well.

So, each man, in turn, rebuked Job for imagined sins, urging him to confess and forsake them if he wished to be restored to health and prosperity. As Job persistently maintained his innocence and his complete ignorance as to why God should deal with him in this way, their arguments and accusations became more insistent and hysterical. If Job really was innocent, where was their own security?

They kept returning to the theme of the evil spirit's message. Even if Job really had not sinned, he had no right to imply that God was unjust, as they thought he was doing. Eliphaz said, for example: "What is man, that he should be clean? and he which is born of a woman, that he should be righteous? Behold, he putteth no trust in his saints; yea, the heavens are not clean in his sight. How much more abominable and filthy is man, which drinketh iniquity like water?" (Job 15:14-16).

These words reflect the truth of God's primeval curse, but even more directly they restate the cynical message of Eliphaz's night visitor. Like the latter, they say nothing of God's redemptive grace.

Finally, unable to shake Job's testimony of innocence, the final discourse of the three friends abandons entirely the charge that Job had willfully sinned. In the shortest of all their eight discourses, Bildad rested their case on the spirit's claim of man's worthlessness. "How then can man be justified with God? or how can he be clean that is born of a woman? Behold even to the moon, and it shineth not; yea, the stars are not pure in his sight. How much less man, that is a worm? and the son of man, which is a worm?" (Job 25:4-6).

Instead of bringing him words of comfort and encouragement, Job's friends brought accusations and words of hopeless despair. No wonder Job said: "I have heard many such things: miserable comforters are ye all" (Job 16:2).

Instead of helping him, they had succeeded only in convicting themselves. If he really had not sinned, as he claimed, they were no better than he. Therefore, they also would have little hope of their own.

They had succeeded, however, in goading Job almost to the breaking point, almost forcing him to accuse God of injustice, though he still maintained his faith. This was the most severe test yet, worse even than the privation and pain. He no longer had even the respect of his closest friends. He who had been so upright now stood accused by those who knew him best, of being a vile sinner. Not only this, but they could offer him no hope. All he could look forward to was death, and even that eluded him. Yet he retained his faith and confidence in God!

The Gospel According to Job

The solution offered by Eliphaz, Bildad, and Zophar to the problem of undeserved suffering was that it *was* deserved. Special suffering is the result of special sin, either known or secret. If that is not the answer, there is no moral order at all. Man is a hunk of clay and will soon be gone altogether.

We must not forget, however, that this is not the right answer. Not only did Job say this was wrong, but so did God! (Job 42:7).

Sin does have consequences, however, and sometimes they are immediate and harsh (such as being jailed for theft, being injured while driving under the influence of alcohol, or contracting a venereal disease while committing fornication). But there are countless cases of believers who suffer because of the sins of others (such as being injured by a drunken driver) or for no apparent reason at all.

Job's suffering could not be attributed to anyone's sin, however, neither his own or someone else's. No human being was responsible for the deadly tornado and no carrier transmitted to him the fearful afflictions that ravaged his body. Neither he nor anyone else (not even God) could rightfully charge him with either overt or secret sin.

Under the taunts and accusations of his friends, Job continually protested his innocence and his mystification. To his friends he pled: "Teach me, and I will hold my tongue:

and cause me to understand wherein I have erred" (Job 6:24). "Make me to know my transgression and my sin" (Job 13:23).

To God he cried: "Do not condemn me; shew me wherefore thou contendest with me" (Job 10:2). "Thou knowest that I am not wicked" (Job 10:7). "If I be wicked, woe unto me; and if I be righteous, yet will I not lift up my head. I am full of confusion; therefore see thou mine affliction" (Job 10:15).

The anguish and sincerity in his soul led him to urge God to examine the records he keeps in heaven: "My prayer is pure. . . . Also now, behold, my witness is in heaven, and my record is on high" (Job 16:17–19).

Because of his insistence on his own moral integrity, many modern writers (as well as his own friends) have charged Job with the sin of pride and self-righteousness. It is clear, however, that he never claimed to be sinless. He knew as well as his friends did that all men are born sinners. In reference to this fact, he said: "Who can bring a clean thing out of an unclean? not one" (Job 14:4). "What is man, that thou shouldest magnify him? and that thou shouldest set thine heart upon him?" (Job 7:17). "How should man be just with God?" (Job 9:2).

In addition to recognizing his basic sinful nature and the barrier this imposed between all men and God, Job was willing to confess and forsake any particular acts of sin he might have committed, if only his friends would tell him what they were. Since he himself did not know of any, and since he had conscientiously tried to live as he believed God wanted him to live, it would have been a lie to say otherwise, and that itself would have been a sin!

As God liveth, who hath taken away my judgment; and the Almighty, who hath vexed my soul; All the while my breath is in me, and the spirit of God is in my nostrils; My lips shall not speak wickedness, nor my tongue utter deceit. God forbid that I should justify you: till I die I will not remove mine integrity from me. My righteousness I hold fast, and will not let it go: my heart shall not reproach me so long as I live (Job 27:2–6).

We must not forget that God himself testified that Job was a perfect and an upright man.

Remember, too, that Job regularly had offered sacrifices as an atonement (covering) for any sins he or his family may have committed in ignorance. He was aware that his own righteousness was not sufficient to make him right with a holy God. A sacrificial substitute, dying and shedding its blood upon an altar, was necessary to atone for sin, and had been ever since Adam. Job knew, and obeyed, this great principle. On this basis he could pray:

> I have sinned; what shall I do unto thee, O thou preserver of men? why hast thou set me as a mark against thee, so that I am a burden to myself? And why dost thou not pardon my transgression, and take away mine iniquity? for now shall I sleep in the dust; and thou shalt seek me in the morning, but I shall not be" (Job 7:20–21).

But the heavens were silent, and Job could not understand why God would not hear his prayers. He could not know that this was all a part of the game rules that had been established for the heavenly experiment in which he and his faith were the test objects.

Job apparently sensed, however, that he was being tested for some reason he could not fathom. "He knoweth the way that I take: when he hath tried me, I shall come forth as gold" (Job 23:10). He also had been visited by evil spirits, presumably bearing a message similar to the one sent to Eliphaz. "When I say, My bed shall comfort me, my couch shall ease my complaint; Then thou scarest me with dreams, and terrifiest me through visions: So that my soul chooseth strangling, and death rather than my life" (Job 7:13–15). Job, like Eliphaz, must have assumed his visions came from the Lord, and he could not understand why they were frightening instead of instructive. He sensed that he was being subjected to these strange and terrible trials for some mysterious purpose, but he was completely in the dark as to why, and this was perhaps the greatest attack of all on his faith. "Oh that I knew where I might find him! that I might come even to his seat! I would order my cause before him, and fill my mouth with arguments. I would know the words which he would answer me, and understand what he would say unto me" (Job 23:3–5).

Since he could not reach God directly, he longed for a mediator—someone through whom he could communicate with God. "For he is not a man, as I am, that I should answer him, and we should come together in judgment. Neither is there any daysman betwixt us, that might lay his hand upon us both" (Job 9:32–33). "Oh that one would hear me! behold, my desire is, that the Almighty would answer me, and that mine adversary had written a book" (Job 31:35).

Although God had revealed certain laws to the ancient patriarchs, he had not yet written his Book, so Job knew very little about his plans for eternity or about the cosmic conflict in which he, unknowingly, had become a central figure. He realized that he needed a "daysman," or mediator, to reach God, but anyone who could bridge the gulf between man and God would have to be both God and man, and where could such a God/man ever be found?

Job knew that God had promised a coming Redeemer who would make all things right again in the creation. Perhaps this would be the longed-for daysman.

In the meantime, he hoped for deliverance through death, as his earthly situation seemed beyond any hope.

"O that thou wouldest hide me in the grave, that thou wouldest keep me secret, until thy wrath be past, that thou wouldest appoint me a set time, and remember me!" (Job 14:13). Up to this time in history, God had revealed very little about life after death, and Job seems to have believed that his body would go back to the dust and his soul would simply go to sleep. "For now should I have lain still and been quiet, I should have slept: then had I been at rest" (Job 3:13). "But man dieth, and wasteth away: yea, man giveth up the ghost, and where is he? . . . So man lieth down, and riseth not: till the heavens be no more, they shall not awake, nor be raised out of their sleep" (Job 14:10–12).

These feelings of Job should not be regarded as divinely inspired truth about death, since they contradict later revelation clearly teaching that the souls of believers go to be with Christ in heaven when they die (e.g., 2 Cor. 5:1, 6, 8; Phil. 1:21, 23). They do, however, give us a divinely inspired insight into the heart of Job as he searched and longed for such knowledge.

Even though he did not know where his soul would go at death, he believed in a future resurrection and restoration. Perhaps God had revealed this, or perhaps Job knew instinctively that the God of creation, whom he had served all his life, would not leave his servants without hope. The marvelous creation would be meaningless otherwise. God would be capricious and unjust, and this was impossible. So he raised the question to his friends: "If a man die, shall he live again?" And then immediately answered it. "All the days of my appointed time will I wait, till my change come" (Job 14:14).

Job gave an even more clear and uncompromising affirmation of faith in the resurrection and eternal life a short while later. "For I know that my redeemer liveth, and that he shall stand at the latter day upon the earth: And though after my skin worms destroy this body, yet in my flesh shall I see God: Whom I shall see for myself, and mine eyes shall behold, and not another; though my reins be consumed within me" (Job 19:25–27).

Job obviously did not have as clear an understanding of the gospel as we have from the New Testament—or even from Isaiah and the other prophets of the Old Testament. Nevertheless, he *did* comprehend much more of the true gospel of salvation than his friends did. And he continued firm in his faith through months of physical sufferings, through the bitterness of having his closest friends renounce him as an unrepentant sinner, and even when he had lost all hope of deliverance in this life or even of understanding what purpose all his sufferings might serve.

Many modern commentators conclude that Job finally became bitter against God, accusing Him unjustly as a result of his undeserved and unexplained sufferings.

But this is not so, as we shall see, and as God himself later testified (Job 42:7). It would be hard to find anywhere in the Bible a stronger statement of confident and submissive faith in God than Job uttered when he said: "Though he slay me, yet will I trust him: but I will maintain mine own ways before him. He also shall be my salvation, for an hypocrite shall not come before him" (Job 13:15–16).

Elihu, the Super-spiritual

With all their arguments, Job's three fair-weather friends had been unable to convict him of sin (as they wanted), or to break his faith (as Satan wanted). Finally they sat in silence with Job still maintaining his innocence of any known sin and still strong in faith toward God. He was confused and lonely, unable to understand why God was dealing with him so harshly, but he never wavered in his absolute trust in God, as Satan was pressuring him to do. Even in his final, emotion-filled plea, Job still spoke of God as "the God that is above" and "the Almighty" (Job 31:28, 35). Anyone else undergoing such suffering would surely have lost faith long before this. Multitudes of Christians have abandoned their faith for much less cause than Job had. Yet Job still trusted God.

Satan, however, had one more trick up his sleeve. Elihu was there. Though evidently unacquainted with either Job or the others, he was intensely absorbed in the highly charged scene before him. Apparently he had come out of curiosity. A learned young man interested in theological and philosophical disputations, he was also impressed with his own spiritual insights and was looking for an opportunity to demonstrate them to these older, better known scholars.

Elihu had listened in silence up to this point, but now he jumped into the argument with great enthusiasm. His six-chapter monologue is the longest in the entire book, and a great portion is taken up with his own commendations of his forthcoming counsel. For example:

> Great men are not always wise: neither do the aged understand judgment. Therefore I said, Hearken to me; I also will shew mine opinion.... For I am full of matter, the spirit within me constraineth me.... I will speak, that I may be refreshed:... Behold, now I have opened my mouth, my tongue hath spoken in my mouth. My words shall be of the uprightness of my heart: and my lips shall utter knowledge clearly.... Mark well, O Job, hearken unto me:... hold thy peace, and I shall teach thee wisdom.... Hear my words, O ye wise men, and give ear unto me, ye that have knowledge (Job 32:9–10, 18, 20; 33:2–3, 31, 33; 34:1).

There are many other statements in the same vein. Elihu held a very high opinion of his own spiritual understanding and philosophical insight.

With such a high recommendation from the speaker himself, we are led to expect some new and brilliant revelation that will solve all the problems and conflicts exposed in the earlier chapters. Many commentators, taking Elihu's boasts on their own terms, have argued that he gives a better understanding of the problems than did Job or the other three friends.

Yet when we look closely at his arguments, we find him merely rephrasing the charges made by Eliphaz, Bildad, and Zophar. Furthermore, he seriously distorts Job's testimonies and pleas, ignoring his repeated assertions of trust in God. Elihu also ignored Job's acknowledgment of innate sin, the possibility that he may have sinned unknowingly, and his desire only to be made aware of whatever may have occasioned God's (apparent) sudden hostility.

Elihu argues that Job had sinned by raising questions about God's justice. "For he addeth rebellion unto his sin, he clappeth his hands among us, and multiplieth his words against God" (Job 34:37). Elihu seems even to have distorted Job's words to make his point: "For he hath said, It profiteth a man nothing that he should delight himself with God" (Job 34:9). "Thinkest thou this to be right, that thou saidst, My righteousness is more than God's? For thou saidst, What advantage will it be unto thee? and, What profit shall I have, if I be cleansed from my sin?" (Job 35:2–3).

Job said nothing of the sort. Apparently Elihu was referring to Job's statement in Job 21:15: "What is the Almighty, that we should serve Him? and what profit should we have, if we pray unto Him?" Elihu, however, has taken it out of context. Job was not expressing his own feelings here; he was quoting the sentiments of the wicked, those who "say unto God, Depart from us; for we desire not the knowledge of thy ways" (Job 21:14). In building his case against Job, Elihu resorted to distortion and deception. This fact, together with his untoward boasting and spiritual pride, nullify the credibility of his otherwise pious and correct statements about God.

Elihu's initial charge against Job was as follows: "I have heard the voice of thy words, saying, I am clean without transgression, I am innocent; neither is there iniquity in me. Behold, he findeth occasions against me, he counteth me for his enemy" (Job 33:8–10).

Job truthfully maintained his innocence of any *known* sin, but Elihu failed to acknowledge Job's admissions of inherent sin and possible sins of ignorance. For example, Job had said: "If I justify myself, mine own mouth shall condemn me: if I say, I am perfect, it shall also prove me perverse. Though I were perfect, yet would I not know my soul: I would despise my life" (Job 9:20–21). Although Job would not claim himself to be perfect, God did so testify! (Job 1:8; 2:3).

Elihu, like the others, kept accusing Job of overt and wicked sins, not just the possible sin of questioning God. "What man is like Job, who drinketh up scorning like water? Which goeth in company with the workers of iniquity, and walketh with wicked men" (Job 34:7–8). "Thou hast fulfilled the judgment of the wicked: judgment and justice take hold on thee" (Job 36:17). Just as the three other friends did, Elihu repeatedly insisted that God gave temporal blessings to the righteous and temporal punishments to the wicked. "He withdraweth not his eyes from the righteous:. . . . If they obey and serve Him, they shall spend their days in prosperity, and their years in pleasures. But if they obey not, they shall perish by the sword, and they shall die without knowledge. But the hypocrites in heart heap up wrath: they cry not when he bindeth them. They die in youth, and their life is among the unclean" (Job 36:7, 11–14).

Much of Elihu's lengthy discourse was either a mistatement of Job's arguments or a restatement of the arguments of his three friends. There was, however, one very important addition. Elihu charged that Job's sufferings were not only a punishment for his unacknowledged sins of the past, but a chastisement because he questioned God's justice in connection with his unexplained sufferings.

Then Elihu arbitrarily asserted that God speaks to men (including Job in particular) both by dreams and also by sufferings (Job 33:14–22). Job had, indeed, been terrified by dreams and visions (Job 7:14) in addition to his terrible sufferings, but they had not helped at all in his understanding, instead making him more despondent than ever. At this point, Elihu seems to suggest that he himself, with his inspired counsel, is the mediator for whom Job has been searching. If Job will only confess and forsake his sins in the way Elihu has advised, he says that Job will be healed and restored:

> If there be a messenger with him, an interpreter, one among a thousand, to shew unto man his uprightness: Then he is gracious unto him, and saith, Deliver him from going down to the pit: I have found a ransom. His flesh shall be fresher than a child's: he shall return to the days of his youth: He shall pray unto God, and He will be favourable unto him: and he shall see his face with joy: for he will render unto man his righteousness. He looketh upon men, and if any say, I have sinned, and perverted that which was right, and it profited

Perpetuated but distorted the "redeemer"
stole the identity. Semiramis)

me not; He will deliver his soul from going into the pit, and his life shall see the light (Job 33:23–28).

This is a remarkable passage which, if taken out of context, sounds almost like a Messianic prophecy. Many commentators, in fact, have so interpreted it. But the context and the tenor of Elihu's discourse seem to make such an interpretation most inappropriate. Unlike true prophets, Elihu is boastful and inordinately insistent that his counsel be accepted as from God. Referring first to Job's plea for a mediator between him and God, Elihu answered: "Behold, I am according to thy wish in God's stead: I also am formed out of the clay" (Job 33:6). Then, after the above declamation, he ordered: "If thou hast any thing to say, answer me: speak, for I desire to justify thee. If not, hearken unto me: hold thy peace, and I shall teach thee wisdom" (Job 33:32–33).

Satan's Final Assault on Job

This brash and arrogant attitude of a novice theologian to a godly and respected patriarch undergoing unexplained sufferings seems inexcusable, especially when he had misunderstood (or perhaps distorted) what Job had said. Yet he seemed to think he was divinely inspired in his pronouncements. Obviously speaking about himself, he claimed: "There is a spirit in man: and the inspiration of the Almighty giveth them understanding. Great men are not always wise: neither do the aged understand judgment. Therefore I said, Hearken to me; I also will shew mine opinion. . . . For I am full of matter, the spirit within me constraineth me" (Job 32:8–10, 18).

There is legitimate reason to question, however, whether this constraining spirit within him was God's Holy Spirit or some alien spirit seeking to use Elihu to destroy Job's faith.

Eliphaz had likewise been deceived by such a spirit, and Job himself had been terrified by them in dreams and visions. Yet Job maintained his faith through it all. In fact, as this climactic day and its arguments progressed, Job's trust in God seemed to grow even stronger. His apparent questioning of God's justice had been, in reality, a defense of God, not an attack.

Knowing that he had conscientiously sought to honor the Lord in thought, word, and deed—even during months of privation and suffering—Job could not honestly confess otherwise. He knew that God knew this also, and he could only resign himself to the confidence that God, for some reason not yet revealed, was trying him, as gold refined through fire (Job 23:10).

Looking more closely at Elihu's pseudo-Messianic claims, we can perhaps discern the outlines of Satan's final attack on Job's faith. Elihu had suggested to Job that God would send "a messenger with him, an interpreter, one among a thousand" (Job 33:23), if he would just confess his sins. This messenger would then prevail upon God to "deliver his soul from going into the pit" (Job 33:28), saying: "I have found a ransom" (Job 33:24).

In this passage, the word for *messenger* is the same as *angel*. It could refer either to a human messenger or to an angel, either a heavenly angel or one of the fallen angels. Elihu evidently thought he himself was the heaven-sent messenger. The word for *ransom* is the same as for *atonement* or better, *covering*. Nowhere, however, does Elihu mention that the true ransom for sin must be the shed blood of an innocent substitute, and he was certainly not offering himself in that capacity! Job did know this, however, as shown by his regular sacrifices on behalf of himself and his family. All Elihu offered was advice! He considered himself "one in a thousand," in terms of spiritual insight and theological understanding.

The word for *interpreter* is particularly interesting. It is more commonly translated as *scorner* or *mocker*, and is not the usual word used for interpreting meanings (e.g., of dreams). This kind of interpretation, done for someone unable to understand on his own, is done with some degree of

condescension or scorn on the part of the interpreter. It may
have been appropriate for Elihu to classify himself as an
interpreter of this sort, but not as a true messenger from the
Lord.

All in all, Elihu's message to Job was not helpful at all. If
successful, he could only have driven Job away from God.
Eliphaz, Bildad, and Zophar had tried to convince Job that
his sufferings were divine punishment because of his sins,
but they had done this by fallacious reasoning that Job
easily repudiated. Elihu tried to do the same thing, but
he claimed that his message came directly from God, and
added the tempting offer of renewed health and prosperity
if Job would only confess to sins that Job knew were non-
existent.

This was a vicious dilemma. If Elihu were really speaking
words from God, as he claimed, then God was asking Job to
confess to what both he and God knew was a lie, and such a
"god" could not be the God Job had trusted and obeyed all
his life. Yet how could he charge Elihu with being a liar? He
seemed sincere, and he spoke with genuine knowledge of
God's creation and in expressions of apparent deep piety.

This was surely a master stroke of Satanic deception.
Elihu was an intelligent, spiritually minded young man who
probably was unaware that he was being manipulated in
such a way. Much of what he says is true and helpful,
especially his eulogy of God's creative handiwork and providential ordering of his creation (Job 36:26 – 37:24).

The reason he was so susceptible to Satanic deception and
confusion, while still so self-confident in his role of divine
messenger, may have been simply the arrogance of gifted
youth. This is why the apostle Paul cautioned Timothy to be
careful in selecting pastoral leaders and teachers. They
must be sufficiently mature, "one that ruleth well his own
house, . . . Not a novice, lest being lifted up with pride he fall
into the condemnation of the devil" (1 Tim. 3:4–6).

In any case, this terrible dilemma facing Job climaxed
months of unparalleled suffering and a day of depressing

argumentation and final rejection by his closest friends. He could neither confess to non-existent sins (for that would deny his God of truth) nor deny that God could send the messenger for which he had prayed (for that also would deny God), and here was Elihu in all sincerity claiming to be such a messenger.

Consequently, Job did not answer Elihu at all! And by choosing not to do so, he did not deny God, as Satan had predicted and tried to get him to do. Furthermore, with this deception, Satan had gone too far. He had tried to maneuver Job into such a position that he would have no choice but to deny God.

It was time, therefore, for God finally to break His silence. Job had "kept the faith," in spite of the worst Satan could do, so the contest was over, and we hear no more of Satan nor of his arguments.

Nevertheless, there is some unfinished work for God to accomplish in the heart of Job and in the lives of his three well-meaning but self-justifying friends. This brings us to the climax of the book and the heart of its message—the magnificent two-fold discourse from none other than the God of creation.

6

The Healing Message of Creation

After months of terrible sufferings, made even worse by the seeming abandonment by the God he had loved and served all his life, Job had now been rejected and accused of wickedness and hypocrisy by his closest friends. Finally, near the close of this bitterest day of his life, he had endured a lengthy diatribe by an arrogant young man who professed to have a direct message of condemnation of him from God Himself. He had longed for some kind of word from God, or even from a God-sent "daysman," but he felt that Elihu's message could not really be that message, despite Elihu's obvious intelligence and spiritual motivation. There seemed nothing more that Job could say.

God finally answered Job's cries—not through an intermediary, but by direct revelation, coming in a mighty whirlwind and bringing a most amazing message. The cosmic drama initiated by Satan's challenge to God's testimony concerning Job's righteousness was almost over. Job had emerged victorious over all the tests Satan could devise and had vindicated God's proposal. Satan and the entire heavenly host had witnessed this demonstration of the efficacy of God's saving grace. God's "scientific hypothesis" had stood up under the most severe "falsification tests" that Satan could devise.

Though songs of victory may have been resounding in the heavens, there was still the unfinished business of Job's vindication on earth and the vindication of God's own moral order in the confused minds of those who had counseled Job when they themselves had been deceived.

The four-chapter message direct from God that climaxes the Book of Job is unparalleled by anything else in the Bible. Even unbelieving scholars acknowledge it as one of the world's greatest masterpieces of literature. As we shall see, however, it is much more than that. It enables us to understand God's great love and his eternal purposes in a unique, though somewhat disconcerting and surprising way. It also provides the long-needed key to effective and victorious living under circumstances of pain and sorrow.

The Witness of Creation

Through the day of traumatic confrontation, Job, his friends, and Elihu, had wrestled with the great problem of undeserved suffering. This problem, addressed philosophically and theologically by every generation, has come to little resolution. It is perhaps the most difficult of all human problems, both because of its intellectual mysteries and its experiential agonies. It probably is the most common of all excuses given by men and women for renouncing belief in a God of love and power.

The problem comes to its sharpest focus in the testing of Job and the intense, probing dialogue between him and his friends. The solution championed by Eliphaz, Bildad, and Zophar involved Job in secret sinning and unrelenting hypocrisy. Although this explanation may be correct in some cases, it is not always true, and it certainly was not true in Job's case. Both Job and God vigorously denied this charge (Job 42:7).

Elihu repeated the charges with what some think was a slightly different twist, suggesting that God was using Job's sufferings as a chastening device, for instructional purposes. For example, Elihu urged Job to respond as follows: "I have borne chastisement, I will not offend any more: That which I see not teach thou me: if I have done iniquity, I will do no more" (Job 34:31-32).

Job had repeatedly spoken words to the same effect, but Elihu ignored them. Job did not know of any way in which he had failed to do God's will, but he was anxious to learn about it if he had. The fact is, Job's sufferings were not to teach him what was wrong in his life, but to teach Satan what God's grace can accomplish in a human life dedicated to serving the Lord.

Since God did not rebuke Elihu as he did Job's three friends, some commentators suggest that Elihu's message was basically correct. As discussed in the preceding chapter, however, Elihu's message was both arrogant, purporting falsely to be from God, and grossly misleading. The fact that God did not refer to it suggests not that it was right, but that it did not merit recognition. Although God did not specifically repudiate it, neither did he commend or even acknowledge it.

The only passing reference to it is found in God's opening question to Job: "Who is this that darkeneth counsel by words without knowledge?" (Job 38:2). Elihu had claimed to have a message direct from God for Job, but then God acted as though he did not even know Elihu! This was a rhetorical question, for God is omniscient, but it makes it obvious that Elihu didn't know what he was talking about. Unfortunately the same teachers who eulogize Elihu argue that these words were intended for Job. This is impossible, however, for it was Elihu—not Job—who had been speaking at great length just before God interrupted him out of the whirlwind. Furthermore, God later testified that what Job had said was "right;" he had not spoken "words without knowledge." The question, "Who is this . . . ?" was addressed to Job, of course, because God knew Job, but it was *about* Elihu.

The solutions offered by Job's three friends and by Elihu to the problem of suffering, whether punishment for sin or chastisement for instruction, were inadequate solutions and, in Job's case, completely wrong. Job himself had no solution and desperately appealed to God to provide one while steadfastly maintaining his faith in God and in an ultimate resolution.

So, then, what is God's solution? When he finally enters the dialogue himself, what does he say about this vexing problem of human suffering—especially about suffering that has no obvious relation to the sin of the afflicted one? What a great help it would be as we witness to skeptics and atheists if we had a convincing, satisfying answer to this mystery. People say that the Book of Job was written to solve this problem, so what does God have to say about it?

Amazingly, God says nothing about it! His divine message, given out of the whirlwind, occupies 123 verses in four chapters, yet there is not a word about the sufferings of Job, or even about human suffering in general.

What God does talk about is creation! The mighty message from heaven focuses exclusively on the doctrine of special creation of all things by God, and then his providential care of his creation. It exalts his power, his wisdom, his purpose, his love.

This seems very surprising at first, but the reason it seems surprising is that, in our present humanistic culture, even Christians have become self-centered instead of God-centered. We emphasize personal Christianity, personal experience, self-image, inter-personal relationships, and what Jesus can do to meet our needs. All these have their place in the Christian life, but not when they relegate God and his purpose in creation to only a peripheral role in our thoughts and deeds.

It is not that Job and his counselors doubted the truth of creation or God's wisdom and power in it; they repeatedly referred to aspects of creation. Note, for example, the words of Eliphaz (Job 5:9–10), Bildad (Job 25:2–5), Zophar (Job 11:7–9), and especially Elihu (Job 36:26–37:24). Job, of course, had more to say about creation than any of them (Job 9:4–10; 12:16–25; 26:6–14; 28:1–28). It is not that the truth of creation was not recognized by Job and his friends. In fact, there is probably more about the creative and providential works of God in Job than in any other book of the Bible.

Why, then, should this be the sole theme of God's response to the philosophical and theological disputation of Job and his counselors? God's response, at first, seems inadequate when these believers were groping for answers to great human needs and problems.

God is not capricious, however, and he has good reason for everything he says and does. He was deeply concerned with Job, his suffering, and his reaction to it. Therefore, his reply to Job's pleadings could not have indicated indifference. Instead, silence must have been the best possible answer, both to the wrong solutions proposed by his friends and to Job's confusion as he sought to understand them.

This leads us to the remarkable conclusion that a correct and complete doctrine of creation is the answer to all the problems that burden this present hurting world. Rather than placing too much emphasis on creation, Job and his friends needed to give it more emphasis. Creation should have first priority in their thinking, no matter what problem they were facing. If God himself laid such stress on it in dealing with this most vexing of all human problems, we would also do well to give it priority when dealing with this or lesser problems. Before proceeding with a fuller study of God's message in these chapters, we need to consider the broader scope of biblical revelation on God's creation.

The Vital Importance of Special Creation

Many modern evangelicals believe that Christian creationists stress the doctrine of special creation too much. Even many pastors and Christian leaders who have not adopted a compromise position on origins seem to consider creation so unimportant that they rarely, if ever, preach on it. This is a tragic mistake.

The foundational importance of creation is indicated, first of all, by its primary position in the Bible. The first two chapters of Genesis provide the basic foundation for every other significant doctrine of the Bible. And in Job, the next oldest book of Scripture, we find the Lord placing paramount emphasis on creation as he brings the great drama to its climactic close.

Those who protest that the doctrine of salvation is more important than creation and thus merits greater emphasis, should note that all doctrines related to salvation are directly based on creation. Jesus Christ was the Creator long before he became the Savior, "for by him were all things created, that are in heaven, and that are in earth" (Col. 1:16). Similarly, creation is the foundation of the gospel of our salvation, a fact made especially clear in the last biblical mention of the gospel. "And I saw another angel fly in the midst of heaven, having the everlasting gospel to preach unto them that dwell on the earth, and to every nation, and kindred, and tongue, and people, Saying with a loud voice, Fear God, and give glory to him; . . . and worship him that made heaven, and earth, and the sea, and the fountains of waters" (Rev. 14:6–7). This "everlasting gospel" centers on worshiping God as Creator of all things. The Scriptures give a sober warning against following even "an angel from heaven" if he should "preach any other gospel" than the gospel preached by Paul (Gal. 1:8), so there can be no doubt that the gospel preached by the angel of Revelation is the same gospel of Christ that Paul preached.

Similarly, the faith in Christ by which we are saved and by which we live is, first of all, faith in special creation. This is made clear in Hebrews 10:38–11:3. Those who are "just [i.e., justified or declared righteous by God] shall live by faith" (Heb. 10:38), for these "believe [i.e., have faith] to the saving of the soul" (Heb. 10:39). This living, saving faith is defined first of all as follows: "Through faith we understand that the worlds were framed by the word of God, so that things which are seen were not made of things which do appear" (Heb. 11:3). Note that this definition precludes the possibility of evolution being "God's method of creation," as many would like to believe. If that were the case, the "things which are seen" would have been made out of pre-existing materials, or "things which appear." True creation is "creation *ex nihilo*," or "creation out of nothing" except the power of the Word of God, which, according to John 1:1–3, 14 is the Lord Jesus Christ.

Thus, genuine creation, instead of being a peripheral doctrine, is absolutely vital to true Christianity. It is the foundation of the gospel of Christ. Furthermore, to know the Lord Jesus Christ as he really is (not as "another Jesus," as in 2 Cor. 11:4 or as some "false Christ," as prophesied in Mark 13:22), we must recognize him as Creator as well as Savior. Finally, saving faith in Christ is, first of all, focused on the truth of the *ex nihilo* creation of all things by Christ. It was appropriate, therefore, that when God finally answered Job, he emphasized the significance of special creation.

Creation is also basic in evangelism and missions, according to the Bible. The one book of the Bible written specifically to lead people to Christ is the Gospel of John. John stated his purpose as follows: "These [signs] are written, that ye might believe that Jesus is the Christ, the Son of God; and that believing ye might have life through his name" (John 20:31). All the great signs of John's Gospel were mighty miracles of supernatural creation (e.g., turning water into wine), accomplishable only by the Creator himself. Most importantly, John *began* his Gospel with an emphasis on creation, starting with the words of Genesis 1:1: "In the beginning was the Word, and the Word was with God, and

the Word was God.... All things were made by him, and
without him was not anything made that was made" (John
1:1–3). If John, whose divinely inspired purpose in writing
was to win people to Christ, began with creation, then so
should others who have the same aim. When people say (as
many do) that we should not be concerned with creation but
only with winning souls for Christ, they don't realize that
this is a contradiction. We must be concerned with creation
if we really want to get people saved and not just sentimen-
tally involved with "another Jesus."

This was the approach followed by the apostles when they
first went out preaching the gospel in obedience to the Great
Commission. Whenever Paul, for example, went into a syna-
gogue, he would open the Scriptures to show that Jesus
had fulfilled the Messianic prophecies. Then he would prove
that Jesus was the long-awaited Redeemer by pointing to
Christ's resurrection from the dead. Note, for example, the
account of his ministry to the Jews in Antioch (Acts 13:14–43)
and Thessalonica (Acts 17:1–3). The Jews already believed
the Scriptures were the Word of God. Therefore, they believed in the true God and in the biblical record of creation,
so the apostles could build on this foundation.

When they went to the pagan Gentiles, however, they were
speaking to people who neither knew nor believed the Bible.
They were all evolutionary pantheists (Stoics, Epicureans,
Gnostics, Platonists, etc.) who believed neither in one supreme personal God nor in special creation. In such cases,
Paul began his preaching by pointing out that the world had
been specially created and that they were responsible, first
of all, to their Creator.

At Lystra, for example, they cried out; "We also are men of
like passions with you, and preach unto you that ye should
turn from these vanities unto the living God, which made
heaven, and earth, and the sea, and all things that are
therein: Who in times past suffered all nations to walk in
their own ways. Nevertheless, he left not himself without
witness, in that he did good, and gave us rain from heaven,

and fruitful seasons, filling our hearts with food and glad-
ness" (Acts 14:15–16).

Similarly, when Paul witnessed to the Greek philosophers
at Athens, he said: "God that made the world and all things
therein, seeing that he is Lord of heaven and earth . . . giveth
to all life, and breath, and all things; And hath made of one
blood all nations of men for to dwell on all the face of the
earth, and hath determined the times before appointed, and
the bounds of their habitation" (Acts 17:24–26).

The reason that men of all times and places need a Savior
and Redeemer is that they are in a state of rebellion against
their Creator; they have "changed the truth of God into a lie,
and worshipped and served the creature [i.e., the world, its
systems, or its created beings] more than the Creator" (Rom.
1:25). This is as true for modern atheists, humanists, Com-
munists, Buddhists, and all other varieties of evolutionists
as it was for the ancient pantheistic evolutionists. Men and
women must first be brought back to a recognition of their
Creator before they can comprehend the meaning of sin
against him and salvation by him.

Still, this is not all. Creation is not only the basis of true
Christology, true faith, and true salvation, but also of true
fellowship and true peace among human beings. Christ has
paid the price, "having made peace through the blood of his
cross, by him to reconcile all things unto himself; by him, I
say, whether they be things in earth, or things in heaven"
(Col. 1:20).

Before people can be truly reconciled to one another, they
must be reconciled to God. Peace on earth among men pre-
supposes peace between men and God. The purpose on earth
of those who have been reconciled to God is to bring others
to the same happy condition. "If any man be in Christ, he is a
new creature [i.e., God has created in him new spiritual life,
by means of the same creative omnipotence with which he
spoke the world into being]: . . . And all things are of God,
who hath reconciled us to himself by Jesus Christ, and hath
given to us the ministry of reconciliation; . . . Now then we

are ambassadors for Christ, as though God did beseech you by us: we pray you in Christ's stead, be ye reconciled to God" (2 Cor. 5:17–20).

With these facts in mind, note the amazing revelation given to the apostle Paul. "By revelation he made known unto me the mystery;. . . Which in other ages was not made known unto the sons of men, . . . That the Gentiles should be fellow-heirs, . . . and partakers of his promise in Christ by the gospel:. . . And to make all men see what is the fellowship of the mystery, which from the beginning of the world hath been hid in God, who created all things by Jesus Christ" (Eph. 3:3–9).

This rich passage tells us that God created all things by Jesus Christ so that all men—Jews and Gentiles alike—might enjoy fellowship together in the gospel of Christ. True fellowship among men and nations can only be achieved through him who created all things, who upholds all things by the word of His power (Heb. 1:3), and who has paid the price "to reconcile all things" (Col. 1:20). Those who receive him as their Redeemer become new creations in Christ, henceforth to live for him in implementing the ministry of reconciliation. Thus, the doctrine of creation is the basic foundation upon which genuine fellowship in Christ must be built.

The Real Purpose of the Book of Job

The above considerations bring us finally to the reason for Job's record. At a deeper level, this must be the reason God allowed Satan to initiate and impose such terrible sufferings upon such a godly man.

The purpose underlying the Book of Job seems to be twofold—one directed heavenward, the other earthward. In the first place, the whole drama had begun with Satan's challenge in heaven in the presence of all the other "sons of God." Therefore, not only Satan and his demonic hosts but also all the holy angels of God must have been following the developments on earth with intense interest.

This, in fact, is a part of God's own purpose in the creation and redemption of men and women on earth. In the same passage that deals with the mystery of God's creation of true fellowship, as cited above, Paul notes this heavenly aspect of our testimony. "And to make all men see what is the fellowship of the mystery, which from the beginning of the world hath been hid in God, who created all things by Jesus Christ: To the intent that now unto the principalities and powers in heavenly places might be known by the church the manifold wisdom of God, According to the eternal purpose which he purposed in Christ Jesus our Lord" (Eph. 3:9–11).

Thus, Job's ordeal and his faithfulness through it was a marvelous testimony—not only to Satan but also to the entire host of heaven—of the glorious effectiveness of God's great plan. It provided tremendous incentive to all the holy angels to serve more faithfully themselves as "ministering spirits" to the "heirs of salvation" (Heb. 1:14). They continue to this day observing with intense interest the outworkings of God's salvation in our own lives, especially in times of stress and trouble. "Of which salvation . . . the angels desire to look into" (1 Peter 1:10–12). Those who have already gone from this life to be with the Lord also are probably deeply concerned observers of our lives on earth. "Wherefore seeing we also are compassed about with so great a cloud of witnesses, let us lay aside every weight, and the sin which doth so easily beset us, and let us run with patience the race that is set before us, looking unto Jesus the author and finisher of our faith; who for the joy that was set before him endured the cross, despising the shame, and is set down at the right hand of the throne of God" (Heb. 12:1–2).

Job's record also had an important earthward testimony, as evidenced by God's magnificent four-chapter message at its conclusion. This message, which said nothing about Job's sufferings nor about the observing hosts in heaven, dealt instead with God's great creation and his providential care over it. Thus, here at the beginning of God's gracious gift of divine revelation to men, in the ancient Book of Job, God

again stressed the importance of the creation he had first
revealed in the opening chapters of Genesis.

In Job's day, most nations were rapidly drifting away
from monotheistic creationism into pantheistic, polytheistic, evolutionary humanism. Even though Job and his
friends still believed in God and frequently referred to his
creation, God indicated the need for a much stronger emphasis to keep the still-believing remnant from drifting into
pagan evolutionism.

That being the case, we can infer that a still stronger
emphasis on creation is needed today, when the intellectual
establishments of almost every nation have repudiated it
and evolutionism reigns supreme in the schools, media,
sciences, and political institutions. Today, as in Communist
nations, blatant atheism often is legislated. The ancient pantheistic evolutionism still dominates such ethnic religions
as Hinduism, Confucianism, Buddhism, Taoism, Shintoism,
and animism. Even in such nominally monotheistic nations
and faiths as Islam, Judaism, and Christianity, evolutionary
humanism and practical atheism seems to control the thinking of their leaders. Most alarming of all, perhaps, is that
even those Christian institutions still giving nominal alle-
giance to Christ and to biblical authority have largely
allowed it to be undermined by such unbiblical (and uns-
cientific) compromises as theistic evolutionism and progres-
sive creationism.

The need, therefore, for a worldwide revival of the doctrine of real creation and a personal Creator God is great.
God's urgent message to Job and his contemporaries is more
vital now than ever before.

God's message spoke directly to the personal needs of Job
and to the "suffering saints" of all times and places. Our
"God of all grace" (1 Peter 5:10) and "God of all comfort"
(2 Cor. 1:3) was certainly not indifferent to the hurts of
his beloved and faithful servant Job. He had heard Job's
prayers, even though Job did not know it. Although God did
not choose to tell Job the reason for his suffering, he did give
Job a way of escape (1 Cor. 10:13).

That way of escape was to recognize and reaffirm God's right, as Creator, to do what he wills with his creatures. "Shall not the Judge of all the earth do right" (Gen. 18:25), whether our time-bound minds can understand his ways or not?

To Job's pleas for understanding God answered, in effect: "Nay but, O man, who art thou that repliest against God? Shall the thing formed say to him that formed it, Why hast thou made me thus?" (Rom. 9:20). "O the depth of the riches both of the wisdom and knowledge of God! how unsearchable are his judgments, and his ways past finding out! For who hath known the mind of the Lord? or who hath been his counselor?" (Rom. 11:33, 34).

Job did not need to know why he was suffering, and neither do we today. God may, in grace, explain in particular cases, but he is under no obligation to do so. In some cases suffering may be punishment for sins or a form of instructional chastisement, and we should prayerfully and submissively examine this possibility. Job's friends and Elihu were correct in insisting that God uses such methods when appropriate, even though they are not the invariable, or even usual, explanation for suffering.

If, like Job, we are called to endure trouble or sorrow, and if, like him, we are confident it is not related to sin, then God's great message to Job will have a healing impact on our own hearts as well.

As we contemplate the magnificence of his great act of creation, his continuing daily works of providence, and his marvelous gift of salvation, we will see our own problems in the perspective of eternity. We can say, with Paul: "Our light affliction, which is but for a moment, worketh for us a far more exceeding and eternal weight of glory" (2 Cor. 4:17). "For I reckon that the sufferings of this present time are not worthy to be compared with the glory which shall be revealed in us" (Rom. 8:18).

We have far better understanding of this today than Job had, for we have Christ's example to guide and encourage us. "For even hereunto were ye called: because Christ also suffered for us, leaving us an example, that ye should follow his steps: Who did no sin, neither was guile found in his mouth: Who, when he was reviled, reviled not again; when he suffered, he threatened not; but committed himself to him that judgeth righteously" (1 Peter 2:21–23).

Later we shall even note some remarkable parallels between the sufferings of Job and those of Christ. For now, however, we need to look in some detail at the majestic message of creation given us by God Himself.

7

God's Science Examination

In view of the significance of creation to all aspects of Christian doctrine and the Christian life, it is important that we examine closely God's monologue on creation and providence in Job 38–41. These are the truths God wanted Job and his counselors to know in ancient times, and we will find that they are even more relevant for our own times.

We have already noted the surprisingly large scientific content of this most ancient Bible book. The great drama of the book as a whole, it was also noted, can be regarded as a cosmic scientific experiment, in which Satan was attempting to disprove God's "scientific hypothesis" (namely, that His salvation really works in the lives of His people) by imposing various "falsification tests" on it, using God's righteous servant Job as the "guinea pig."

As we approach the remarkable array of questions posed by God in his climactic monologue, it is in keeping with the scientific thrust of the book to regard the questions as a sort of science examination given to Job and the others by their Creator.

In these four chapters, we can count about seventy-seven questions. Many are rhetorical questions, which none of the men could answer except by acknowledging that God himself was the answer, or that God alone knew the answer. Yet many seem to be legitimate concerns of scientific research. If properly conducted, such research might yield at least partial answers. In fact, some of the questions *have* been partially answered by such research. This suggests that all the questions could be investigated scientifically, and God's challenging examination can provide incentives to do just that.

God's Primeval Mandate

An additional reason for God's emphasis here on creation may be as a rebuke to all human beings for their failure to implement his primeval "dominion mandate" given in the Garden of Eden to Adam and Eve. This was his very first commandment, and it has never been withdrawn. "Be fruitful, and multiply, and replenish [fill] the earth, and subdue it: and have dominion . . . over every living thing that moveth upon the earth" (Gen. 1:28).

It was God's purpose in creation that men and women should subdue the earth and have dominion over all its creatures. This commission was renewed and extended after the flood. "And God blessed Noah and his sons, and said unto them, 'Be fruitful, and multiply, and replenish the earth. And the fear of you and the dread of you shall be upon every beast of the earth, and upon every fowl of the air, upon all that moveth upon the earth, and upon all the fishes of the sea; into your hand are they delivered'" (Gen. 9:1–2).

This "dominion mandate" was still in effect in Job's day and is still in effect today. It is authorization for all legitimate human enterprises and occupations. To "subdue the earth" and to "have dominion" over all its creatures requires research into the earth's systems and processes. This is what we call *science*. Once these systems and processes are understood, they can be controlled and used for human benefit and God's glory. This is *technology* (engineering, medicine, agriculture, etc.). Transmitting and communicating this information for optimum use is *business* and *commerce*.Teaching them to succeeding generations is *education*. The *fine arts* (music, literature, art, etc.) glorify God's works of creation and salvation and thus help men and women understand and appreciate their spiritual relationships. Most honorable occupations can be included under this primeval commission, as long as they are carried out in the will of God.

From the above analysis we see that science is the foundational enterprise upon which the others must be built. To subdue the earth means, first of all, to understand it. God did not need men and women to do this. Had he so willed, he could have equipped human beings with all knowledge when he created them. By the same token, he does not need men and women to carry out the work of his second great commission—that of preaching the Gospel around the world. He could have had angels do this, or he could have done it himself.

For reasons known only to God, he commissioned the people he created in his own image to carry out both of these great mandates. If we would carry out his mandates properly, we would know and appreciate him and his wonderful works of creation and redemption all the more, and thus would be better prepared for eternal fellowship with him and service for him, for which we were created.

The tragedy is that we have failed miserably in both commissions. Even Job, righteous though he was, had apparently failed in this sphere of his responsibilities. Although he believed in creation, it did not have the highest priority in his thoughts and actions. He was righteous in every moral sense, highly solicitous of his family's spiritual welfare, kind and generous to those in need, a model citizen, and deeply devoted to God. None could find any legitimate fault in him or flaw in his character, and he remained strong and sound in faith even during all his afflictions.

Nevertheless, he had done little to accomplish God's first commandment, or to encourage others to do so. His understanding and appreciation of God's creation was sound, but it was hardly complete, and was relatively low in his personal priorities. And if this was true of godly Job, it was even more true of his friends, and true in a greater degree of the ungodly world at large.

Perhaps this is the major reason God felt it so essential to deal exclusively with this neglected subject instead of with suffering, the topic uppermost in Job's thinking.

Science has made great strides in recent centuries, and it is significant that they came in the context of the Reformation and the Great Awakening. All the great "founding fathers" of science and technology (Newton, Boyle, Pascal, Brewster, etc.) sought to "think God's thoughts after Him" and to do their science "to the glory of God." The same was true in education and the fine arts. Now, however, these fields of study and practice have been taken over by humanists, and the great tragedy is that Christians, by their indifference, have acquiesced in this Satanic takeover.

God, therefore, in his message to Job, also speaks to us, and his message applies more incisively and urgently now than it could have then. People not only fail to give creation high priority (as in the case of Job and his friends) but almost ignore it altogether, in the case of modern Christians, and even repudiate and ridicule it, in the case of the leaders of the modern world, in every area of thought and practice.

Science, which should have been a great testimony to the majesty and grace of God, has become, instead, a device for ignoring and rejecting him. Surely God will not allow this to continue much longer. We should soberly remember the antediluvian world, Babel, and Sodom. How vital it is, therefore, that we consider carefully the testimonies and questions of the Lord in this great dramatic poem of creation.

The World that Then Was

The first set of divine questions had to do with the history of the primeval world. After making it clear that Elihu's lengthy discourse consisted merely of "darkening counsel by words without knowledge," and that God's own words were primarily in response to Job's prayers (Elihu and the other three had offered their opinions, but none had, like Job, expressed the need or desire to hear directly from God), God spoke the following words of profound wisdom.

"Where wast thou when I laid the foundations of the earth? declare, if thou hast understanding. Who hath laid the measures thereof, if thou knowest? or who hath stretched the line upon it? Whereupon are the foundations thereof fastened? or who laid the corner stone thereof; When the morning stars sang together, and all the sons of God shouted for joy?" (Job 38:4–7).

If humans are ever to "subdue the earth" as God commanded, they must understand, first of all, its wonderful origin. Strange and imaginative have been the various cosmogonies invented by ancient pagan evolutionists and modern "scientific" evolutionists. To all such speculations, God rejoins: "How could you possibly know what happened? Were you there?"

The essence of science (knowledge) is observation. The scientific method requires actual measurement, experimentation, prediction, repetition. None of these are possible with the process of origins and development. Scientists may speak of "the science of origins," and develop elaborate systems of cosmogony and historical geology, but apart from divine revelation, they are nothing but speculations at best, blasphemy at worst.

Materialistic scientists depend on their "principle of uniformitarianism," which assumes that "the present is the key to the past." They contend that present geological processes, given enough time, would develop the earth out of a primeval cloud of dust and that present biological processes would develop life out of dead chemicals and develop plants, animals, and people from some primeval simple cell.

This is absurd. No processes of the present have ever been observed doing any such thing, or even moving in the direction to do such things.

If the present is the key to the past, people should realize that only God can accomplish these things. The construction of a relatively simple system such as a building requires an architect to determine the dimensions, a surveyor to establish the lines, and a builder to set the foundations. An infinitely larger and more complex "building" such as Planet Earth would require no less! The random processes of time and chance may destroy a building, but they could never construct one.

If we want to know how the world began, we must get the information from the only source who can tell us. No human observed the process, and no human can repeat the process. Every such naturalistic or pantheistic process that has ever been imagined by human beings contradicts the basic scientific laws of the present (e.g., causality, conservation, entropy), so how could such processes possibly work? God alone established the earth's foundations, stretched its lines, and laid its cornerstone. Furthermore, he did not require aeons of time to do it. "He spake, and it was done" (Ps. 33:9).

Another important event took place at that time that could be known only by revelation. "The morning stars sang together, and all the sons of God shouted for joy." These mighty angels—the same ones mentioned twice in the prologue to the Book of Job—were fascinated observers when God provided firm foundations for the earth, and they rejoiced when it was done, evidently knowing that the earth would be their primary sphere of ministry when God completed his creation. These angels were the "morning stars" in the Hebrew poetic parallel format used here. According to the creation account in Genesis, the physical stars were not created until the fourth day, whereas the solid foundations of the earth had been established on the third day (the earth material, in elemental form, had first been called into existence on the first day).

The reason the angels were called "morning stars," when the stars themselves were not yet in existence, is not specifically revealed, although angels often are symbolized by stars in later Scripture. Perhaps a reasonable suggestion is that just as earth was "given to the children of men" (Ps. 115:16), the stars were provided as angelic residences. Both stars and angels are called "the host of heaven" in the Bible.

Angels are created beings, not eternally existing like God. Since everything in heaven and on earth was created and made in the creation week (Gen. 2:1–3; Ex. 20:8–11), angels most likely were created—along with light—on the first day.

Angels created on 1st Day

Satan and his angels were among the rejoicing sons of God during the first few days of creation. Later, however, sometime after Adam and Eve were created (when everything was still "very good," even in heaven, according to Gen. 1:31), Satan became God's great adversary.

Next, God reminded Job of the great flood. He asked: "Who shut up the sea with doors, when it brake forth, as if it had issued out of the womb? When I made the cloud the garment thereof, and thick darkness a swaddlingband for it, And brake up for it my decreed place, and set bars and doors, And said, Hitherto shalt thou come, but no further: and here shall thy proud waves be stayed?" (Job 38:8–11).

Just as the "present processes" of uniformitarian scientists could never create anything, neither could they ever produce the cataclysmic changes of the flood. The present-day "sea" of the earth, occupying almost three-fourths of the earth's surface, has come from the two great reservoirs of water established by God on the second day of creation week—the primeval matrix of waters that originally sustained and suspended all earthly materials (see Gen. 1:2; 2 Peter 3:5). The "waters above the firmament" (Gen. 1:7) had been separated from the "waters below the firmament"—one in a great canopy of invisible water vapor above the atmosphere; the other in the "great deep," a vast reservoir of pressurized water below the earth's crust. These two came together to produce the great flood. The "fountains of the great deep" (Gen. 7:11) suddenly "brake forth, as if it had issued out of the womb." Almost simultaneously, the "windows of heaven were opened," and great torrents of rain deluged the whole world for forty days. The invisible vapor blanket extending far into space, quickly condensed into a gigantic covering of cloud over the earth, like a great swaddlingband, enveloping the whole earth in thick darkness, then in devastating torrents of water. Everything in the dry land died (Gen. 7:22), and great numbers of marine animals died as well. Of all the land animals and millions of human beings living in the antediluvian world, only those in Noah's ark survived.

The flood and its associated tectonic, volcanic, and other geophysical phenomena could never have been produced by present processes. Thus its cause can never be discovered from present natural forces. Even Christians often fall into the trap of trying to explain the flood by some naturalistic geophysical cause (e.g., asteroid impact, reversal or shifting of earth's axis, slipping crust). But God would say to them: "Were you there?" He has told us the cause, and this dual cause is sufficient.

The tremendous effects of the flood, however, and the overwhelming evidence of special creation are so clearly evident that God, through the apostle Peter, has charged uniformitarians with willful ignorance! (2 Peter 3:3–6). The geological strata and fossil beds all over the world bear irrefutable witness to the fact that "the world that then was, being overflowed with water, perished" (2 Peter 3:6).

In fact, had it not been for God's intervention and providential care of those in the Ark, the whole world would have been destroyed. By another great geophysical upheaval, however, he "brake up" for the flood waters a "decreed place," and they were forever "shut up" in the deep ocean beds opened up to receive them (note Ps.

104:6–9). The earth's isostatic balances now preclude another global deluge.

Thus, God's questions relating to the "historical sciences"
point out that God's Word can provide clear guidance in the
understanding of these ancient phenomena and their effects, but that evolutionary uniformitarianism is wrong as a
guiding principle of science.

This Present World

Beginning with Job 38:12 and continuing for four chapters, God's questions deal with present processes and systems, and these do constitute the proper domain of science
and its commission to subdue the earth. As noted in Chapter
3, a number of these questions have been partially answered
by scientific research. For example, God asked Job about the
rotation of the earth (vv. 12–15), the springs and pathways of
the sea (v. 16), the breadth of the earth (v. 18), the travel-way
of light (v. 19), the way in which light is parted (v. 24), the
"father" of the rain and the "mother" of the ice sheets
(vv. 28–30), the universal nature of physical laws (v. 33) and
the electrical transmission of communications (v. 35). These
phenomena have been partially elucidated by scientific research, although none are yet fully understood. The questions themselves often constitute remarkable anticipations
of modern discoveries, most of which were made by great
creationist scientists of the past (Newton, Maury, Faraday,
Morse, etc.). These men worked to carry out God's primeval
dominion mandate, thinking God's thoughts after him.

Even those phenomena that are partly understood (involv-
ing basic principles of geophysics, hydrology, oceanography, physics, and other sciences), carry with them the
implied question of their origin! Who established Earth's
uniform rotation, and how is it maintained? How was the
hydrological cycle set up? Whence came all these marvelous
laws and phenomena that science now studies? These are
rhetorical questions whose solution is found only in special
creation and the Creator.

There are still some questions on the divine list whose answers have hardly been touched at all by science. For example: "Have the gates of death been opened unto thee? or hast thou seen the doors of the shadow of death?" (38:17). We know only a little about "the treasures of the snow" and "the treasures of the hail" (38:22). What are "the sweet influences of Pleiades?" (38:31). There are many suggestions for fruitful scientific research in this marvelous chapter.

God even challenges us to research man's ability to do research! "Who hath put wisdom in the inward parts? or who hath given understanding to the heart?" (38:36). God has created in human beings a marvelous brain, beyond any question the most complex aggregation of matter in the universe. Physiologists have learned much about its structure and its processes, but nothing whatever about its origin! Neither Job, his friends, nor people today, begin to use this unique attribute of "the image of God" to its full capacity. Job at least knew the answer to this question! "Whence then cometh wisdom? and where is the place of understanding? Behold, the fear of the Lord, that is wisdom; and to depart from evil is understanding" (Job 28:20, 28).

God's first great commission to mankind still needs to be carried out, but most Christians have abandoned the scientific enterprise to the secularists, with devastating results. The world desperately needs to return to a creationist framework of science if we are ever to "subdue the earth" to God's glory as he has commanded.

Man and the Animals

God placed mankind in dominion over the plant and animal kingdom, but sin has marred this relationship. Instead of close harmony, as originally intended, most animals fear and dread man. Many have been ruthlessly exploited, and multitudes of species have become extinct.

It is significant that more of the questions asked by God in his science examination deal with the biological world than with the physical. Furthermore, all of them stress that it is God himself who cares for the animals, an implied rebuke to men and women who have failed in this stewardship.

In Job 38:39–41, God asks questions about animal behavior and animal sustenance, embracing carnivorous animals (e.g., the lion—Job 38:39–40), herbivorous animals (e.g., the horse—Job 39:19–25), birds of prey (e.g., the raven—Job 39:41), and even scavenger birds (e.g., the eagle or vulture—Job 39:27–30).

Extinct animals are also mentioned—most notably the unicorn (Job 39:9–12). The Hebrew word translated *unicorn* in this and other passages is believed by most Hebrew scholars to refer to the huge and fierce aurochs, or wild ox, which inhabited the Middle East and other regions but is now extinct. God also notes the wild goat (Job 39:1), the hind (Job 39:1–4), the wild ass (Job 39:5–8), the peacock (Job 39:13), the ostrich (Job 39:13–18), the hawk (Job 38:26), and even the grasshopper (Job 39:20). By implication, all the other animals can be included in his expressed concern for these twelve representative animals. Later generations of naturalists have been able to learn partial answers to some of these behavioral questions, and many of the great biological scientists of the past (Ray, Linnaeus, etc.) were, like the physical scientists mentioned previously, creationists. Certain animals noted in God's message are of somewhat doubtful identification (e.g., peacock, ostrich) and may even be now-unknown extinct animals, like the unicorn.

In one of his discourses, Job noted that God had created all the animals and that we could learn from them the reality of a Creator (Job 12:7–10). Eliphaz once referred to lions, but only in a passing comparison with the fate of the wicked (Job 4:10–11). Several other passing references to animals are found in the book (Job 6:5; 8:14; 9:26; 10:16; 20:16; 21:10; 24:3, 5; 28:7, 8; 30:1, 29; 31:20; 37:8). None of these, however, show the slightest indication of concern for the animals as a part of God's creation and man's dominion.

Thus, God's lengthy zoology lesson and examination is a sharp rebuke to those who lack knowledge and lack any feeling of responsibility for the remarkable kingdom of animals that God created and for whom he made such amazing provisions in nature.

A beautiful parallel passage is found in Psalm 104, which first speaks of creation and the flood (vv. 1–9) in similar fashion to the first portion of God's message to Job. The rest of the psalm (vv. 10–35) is a hymn of God's providential care for all his creation. Furthermore, when Jesus Christ came into the world, his manger-bed was surrounded with the animals he had created. He later said: "Are not five sparrows sold for two farthings, and not one of them is forgotten before God?" (Luke 12:6). "Into your hand are they delivered," God told Noah, yet how little most of us (even including Job) seem to care!

In God's message to Job (and to us), eight verses deal with the early history of the earth, twenty-seven with the physical world as it functions today, and thirty-three verses with the nature and needs of the animals (not including the behemoth and the leviathan, which are treated in more detail than the others and which we discuss in the next chapter). All of these are a part of God's creation, giving clear testimony of his omniscience and omnipotence, his providential care for all his creatures, and an implied rebuke to men and women for failing to understand all this.

Furthermore, with God's detailed reminder of how he cares for his creation, especially the animals, there is also a gentle rebuke to Job for thinking that God might have forgotten him! As the Lord Jesus said, just after he had noted that not even a sparrow could "fall on the ground without your Father" (Matt. 10:29), we should remember that "the very hairs of your head are all numbered" (Matt. 10:30) and that "ye are of more value than many sparrows" (Matt. 10:31).

Therefore, God's central message to Job, and to us, is not an explanation of why the righteous suffer, but rather a call to sound belief in creation and an emphasis on our stewardship over that creation, under God. Afflictions that come our way can then be placed in proper context. We belong to him, both by creation and by redemption, and he has the right to do with us whatever he will. We can trust him, no matter what comes our way in this life, knowing that in the balances of eternity the Judge of all the earth will do right.

8

Dragons, Dinosaurs, and the Devil

In addition to the twelve representative animals discussed by God in his creation message to Job, two other animals are described. Behemoth and Leviathan have more space devoted to them (forty-four verses) than the other twelve combined. These are mysterious animals, whose described characteristics correspond to no known living animals. The obvious question, therefore, is why would God devote so much attention to these two fearsome animals in this concluding and climactic portion of his great message.

Job's Rebuke

Before continuing with his zoology exam, however, God paused to speak directly to Job. This interruption indicates that something significant is about to be introduced.

111

The interruption is rather surprising in itself. Job had withstood the charges made by Eliphaz, Bildad, Zophar, and Elihu, all the while insisting in all good conscience, that he was innocent of known sin. Furthermore, God had also declared him to be the most righteous man in the earth. Throughout his terrible ordeal, Job had maintained an un- shaken faith in God until the moment God came in the whirlwind. Soon he would hear God confirm that the accu- sations of his friends had been wrong and that what he himself had said was right (Job 42:7).

Yet here we suddenly find God rebuking Job. "Shall he that contendeth with the Almighty instruct him? he that reproveth God, let him answer it" (Job 40:1). How are we to understand this question suddenly injected here into God's science exam?

It almost seems that this question is the climactic ques- tion of the exam. Even though Job was the most godly man in the world at the time, he had been unable to answer any of God's questions. He should have been able to answer them, if he had been more diligent in carrying out God's primeval commandment with respect to his creation, as given to the first man (Gen. 1:28).

Instead, Job (even before his testing) had been too pre- occupied with his own personal affairs and with those of his family and community to think very often of God's purpose in creation. Lest we find fault with Job in this, we should remember that we ourselves are far more guilty than he in this regard. Job had been careful to keep all God's other commandments as he knew them at the time (Job 23:12), but he had largely forgotten this first commandment! And so have we today.

All of this must have been driven home to Job with great force as God reminded Job repeatedly with his questions, how concerned he was with his creation, even if men and women were not. Among Job's final words were these: "Oh that one would hear me! behold, my desire is, that the Almighty would answer me, and that mine adversary had written a book" (Job 31:35). This challenge could not go unanswered.

In view of God's wonderful care over his physical and biological creations, it was out of line for Job (or anyone else) to assume that God was not concerned about the needs of the ones he had created in his own image. Job's patience, exhibited beautifully under all his afflictions, had finally broken under the unwarranted mental and spiritual attacks. Twice he cried out impatiently for an opportunity to present his case to God (as though God did not already know everything about it!). "Oh that I knew where I might find him! that I might come to his seat! I would order my cause before him, and fill my mouth with arguments" (Job 23:3–4).

At the close of his eight discourses, Job calls God his "adversary." Job did not use this term to mean enemy but prosecuting attorney, one who should have written a "book," or list of the charges against him. If he had done this, Job maintained, he could use it to justify himself. "I would declare unto him the number of my steps; as a prince would I go near unto him" (Job 31:37).

His attitude was thus becoming so desperate as to border on presumption. But that was not all. He then, in effect, called on God to bring the primeval curse on his own land if God could find any unrighteousness in him. His final words had been: "Let thistles grow instead of wheat, and cockle instead of barley. The words of Job are ended" (Job 31:40).

This Edenic Curse, however, had already been pronounced on all men, Job included. Job realized this fact, and had acknowledged it more than once, even offering regular sacrifices in atonement for the unknown sins of himself and his family. He had, more than once, acknowledged God's right to take away what he had given and to send evil as well as good on his people (Job 1:21; 2:10). Finally, however, under these latest spiritual torments, he had apparently forgotten that God's previous blessings had been entirely by God's grace and that the curse was already in effect everywhere.

God loved Job dearly and knew that Job's faithfulness through suffering would vindicate that love, but he could

not permit this attitude to develop any further. After allow-
ing young Elihu to deliver his own harangue (which God
later called "words without knowledge"), he told Job that
before he could presume to interrogate God he should be
able to answer God's own questions to him.

"Then Job answered the LORD, and said, Behold, I am vile;
what shall I answer thee? I will lay mine hand upon my
mouth. Once have I spoken; but I will not answer: yea, twice;
but I will proceed no further" (Job 40:3–5).

When we, like Job, are confronted with the majesty and
intricacy of God's creation, with the marvelous creative
purpose that all this implies, our own problems will become
insignificant and our own complaints and questions will
become frivolous. We do not have to know why God does
every thing he does. What he does is right, by definition! The
proper response is implicit confidence in his goodness and
in his Word. As Job said earlier: "Though he slay me, yet will
I trust in Him" (Job 13:15). He who made the infinite universe can be nothing less than omnipotent; he who designed
the intricate interrelationships of the creation can be nothing less than omniscient; and he who cares so graciously for
all his creatures is a God of perfect love. No questions we
can raise about his actions or judgments can nullify these
truths, and we should leave them for him to answer in
eternity if he so wills.

Pressing home this lesson, God made sure that Job understood what he was saying: "Wilt thou condemn me, that thou
mayest be righteous?" (Job 40:8). Unintentionally, Job was
arrogating to himself the attributes of deity, presuming to
evaluate the morality of God's dealings with his own creatures. We ourselves fall easily into the same Satanic trap if
we are not continually and consciously submissive to God's
Word. He would challenge us, like Job, to put on first all the
attributes of God's glory and then be ready to exercise God's
wrath on those who are proud of heart. Arrogance is the
same sin that the Devil exhibited, and which God must judge
in us as well. If you can do all this, God told Job, "then will I

also confess unto thee that thine own right hand can save thee" (Job 40:14).

Job was humiliated and speechless after this rebuke from God. He could no longer defend his own righteousness, though everything he had said earlier about it was true. He could only acknowledge his own vileness in the presence of his Creator, and wait for further instruction. God proceeded with an unexpected and amazing revelation about the greatest animals in all creation—Behemoth and Leviathan.

Behemoth

God now directs Job's attention to the greatest animals of all, the behemoth on the land and the leviathan in the sea. First there is behemoth. "Behold now behemoth, which I made with thee. . . . He is the chief of the ways of God" (Job 40:15, 19).

Scholars have labored to identify this animal. The word seems to mean gigantic beast, so commentators generally have decided it must be an elephant, hippopotamus, or rhinoceros.

The problem with such an identification is that it doesn't fit. No known living animals conform to the following characteristics: "Lo now, his strength is in his loins, and his force is in the navel of his belly. He moveth his tail like a cedar: the sinews of his stones are wrapped together. His bones are as strong pieces of brass; his bones are like bars of iron. . . . Behold, he drinketh up a river, and hasteth not: he trusteth that he can draw up Jordan into his mouth, . . . his nose pierceth through snares" (Job 40:16–18, 23, 24).

The reason commentators are unable to identify this mighty animal is that it is now extinct. Modern Bible scholars, for the most part, have become so conditioned to think in terms of the long ages of evolutionary geology that it never occurs to them that mankind once lived in the same world with the great animals that are now found only as fossils.

The Bible teaches clearly that all animals, living or extinct, were made on the fifth and sixth days of creation week, along with man, who was given dominion over them (note Gen. 1:20; Exod. 20:8–11). Although most of the earth's great fossil graveyards were formed by the flood, representatives of each animal "kind" in the dry land were preserved on Noah's ark to repopulate the world after the flood (it can be shown that the ark could easily hold two of each known species of land animal, both living and extinct).

Thus, Job and his contemporaries could easily have seen many kinds of animals that later became extinct due to the earth's more rigorous climate and vastly depleted resources after the flood. The behemoth, however, was identified by the Lord as "the chief of the ways of God," indicating that he was the largest of all land animals. Almost certainly, therefore, God was speaking of a mighty dinosaur. The description does fit certain dinosaurs, but no other animals that we know of. The popular evolutionary myth that dinosaurs became extinct about seventy million years before man "evolved" is fallacious, both biblically and scientifically. God made the behemoth with man, God assured Job.

But why would God call special attention at this point to a mighty dinosaur? The divine message continues to emphasize God's great power in creation, and this animal was far greater than any previously mentioned. The dinosaurs were not only the largest, but also the most hideous and fearsome, of all the animals. Although they shared God's providential care for all animals, they also must have inspired great fear and probably loathing in ancient man. Therefore, they would have served effectively as a symbol of evil, probably giving rise to all the tales of dragons that have come down from almost every nation.

Despite the fact that no man could trap one of these beasts, God assured Job that "he that made him can make his sword to approach unto him" (Job 40:19). Before they could proliferate in such numbers as to threaten human survival, God would see to it that they would either die out, or possibly be driven deep into the jungle swamps by need of food, water, and warmth. Modern scientists have long been mystified by the extinction of the dinosaurs, but God was equal to the task when the proper time arrived.

There was yet another implication to be noted by Job from behemoth. His nature, appearance, and power probably reminded men of the serpent in Eden, who had already caused havoc in the world. By this time, Job may have sensed that his troubles, though allowed by God, did not originate with God. The God of creation, who cared for all the animals he had created, even the behemoth, would not deliberately have inflicted such tribulations on one he loved as much as Job. Job may have been thinking by this time that, in some way he could not yet understand, the malignant serpent, symbolized by the ugly dinosaur, was behind it all. Therefore, God's assurance that he could destroy this gigantic beast ought to have given Job a glimmer of hope that his own sufferings might soon be over—if he recalled God's Edenic promise that the Serpent would one day be destroyed (Gen. 3:15).

Leviathan

The witness of the great beast behemoth is brought into still sharper focus when God begins to speak of leviathan. As the behemoth was the greatest terrestrial animal, the leviathan was the greatest aquatic animal. Like the behemoth, it seems to be extinct, although reports continue to persist of great sea serpents and plesiosaur-like animals in oceans and deep lakes around the world.

Most commentators, once again limiting their thinking to existing animals, insist on calling the leviathan a crocodile. Once again, however, the awesome description in Job 41 does not fit at all. Whatever the leviathan may have been, it was not a crocodile! Neither was it a whale, as some have suggested, even though whales are the largest animals living today. Note a few characteristics of leviathan.

"Canst thou fill his skin with barbed irons? or his head with fish spears?. . . Behold, the hope of him is in vain: shall not one be cast down even at the sight of him? None is so fierce that dare stir him up:. . . The sword of him that layeth at him cannot hold" (Job 41:7, 9, 10, 26). These and other verses indicate that the leviathan was impregnable to human efforts to capture or slay him. Yet zoos are full of crocodiles, and crocodiles have been hunted so successfully that they are often considered an endangered species. The same applies to whales.

And what about the following description? "By his neesings a light doth shine, and his eyes are like the eyelids of the morning. Out of his mouth go burning lamps, and sparks of fire leap out. Out of his nostrils goeth smoke, as out of a seething pot or caldron. His breath kindleth coals, and a flame goeth out of his mouth" (Job 41:18–21).

This is surely not a crocodile! To the possible objection that not even dinosaurs breathed fire, we could answer that no one *knows* what dinosaurs could do.

Dragons of various kinds were capable of breathing out fire—at least according to traditions from all parts of the world. Certain insects can, in effect, give out light or fire (e.g., the bombardier beetle and the firefly), as can various luminescent fish. Perhaps more to the point, dinosaur fossils have been excavated that show a strange protuberance, with internal cavity, on the top of the head. It is conceivable that this could have served as a sort of mixing chamber for combustible gases that would ignite when exhaled into the outside oxygen.

In any case, it seems unlikely that the ubiquitous tales of fire-breathing dragons in ancient times, coming as they do from all parts of the world, could have come into existence without a strong factual basis. Furthermore, the Bible often mentions dragons just as it mentions unicorns—always in such a way as to show that the writers believed they were real animals.

For example, the first mention of the animal creation refers to such animals. "God created great whales" (Gen.

1:21). The word translated *whales* in the King James is often translated *sea monsters* in other versions. In most other passages, however, the word is translated *dragons* or sometimes *serpents*. It apparently was meant to identify the animal called a dragon in other nations.

The leviathan is specifically identified as a dragon in one biblical text, where it is called "leviathan . . . the dragon that is in the sea" (Isa. 27:1).

That it is not a mythical creature is clearly asserted in the great psalm of God's providence. When the psalmist speaks of "that great and wide sea" in which there are "things creeping innumerable," he also notes that "there is that leviathan, whom thou hast made to play therein" (Ps. 104:25, 26). The description in Job also notes that "he maketh the deep to boil like a pot" (Job 41:31).

The leviathan was a real animal, presumably the largest and fiercest of all the aquatic dinosaurs. Like the behemoth, however, he also symbolized the great power and pride of the wicked one, Satan. This is even more evident in this case than for behemoth. Some of the divine references to leviathan could not literally apply to any animal, even this one. They could, in fact must, apply ultimately to Satan, and to him alone.

As we read Job 41, it seems that we alternately read about a powerful animal and a more powerful malevolent spirit, as though God were describing both leviathan and Satan intermittently but in the same context. The following statements and phrases, for example, though referring directly to the great animal, seem also to personify him as evil.

Will he make many supplications unto thee? will he speak soft words unto thee? Will he make a covenant with thee? wilt thou take him for a servant for ever? . . . Behold, the hope of him is in vain: shall not one be cast down even at the sight of him? . . . When he raiseth up himself, the mighty are afraid: . . . Upon earth there is not his like, who is made without fear (Job 41:3–4, 9, 25, 33).

The conclusive verse in this connection is the last verse of God's message to Job: "He beholdeth all high things: he is king over all the children of pride" (Job 41:34). Such a statement could not be true of any animal, but it could be true of Satan. In fact, it could be literally applicable *only* to Satan.

Satan, that old serpent, the Devil—it is he and he alone who is the king of all the proud ones, for he is the father of all the children of pride. Only Satan has beheld all high things. He once was God's anointed cherub, the highest of all the angels, but he wanted to exalt his own throne above the throne of God, and God had to cast him out. The story is told more fully in Isaiah 14:12–15 and Ezekiel 28:11–19.

It is interesting to note the use of parallel meanings in these passages. The Isaiah passage is addressed both to the wicked king of Babylon and to the wicked one controlling him. The Ezekiel passage is addressed ostensibly to the evil king of Tyre but soon passes beyond him to the indwelling Satan. In Job, God's description of the fearful dragon, leviathan, likewise applies more fully to Satan, who apparently was possessing *his* body, just as he had once used the *serpent's* body back in the Garden of Eden.

Looking behind the scenes, and reading between the lines, we can surely discern the presence of Satan here at this final confrontation. Satan's pride and arrogant challenge of God in the heavenly gathering had initiated this entire drama. At the end of the drama, Satan is bound to be present somewhere, somehow, in some form.

Whether Job actually saw behemoth and leviathan, the account does not fully indicate. God did say to Job, however, "Behold now behemoth" (Job 40:15). Perhaps this means Job could see the animal then. In any case, God was speaking to Job about the animals as though he were in their presence. By this time, Job could probably sense that he was also in the deadly presence of the evil one who had been battling with God for his soul.

Even though no one else could conquer behemoth, God assured Job that God's own sword could reach him. The same was true of leviathan. "None is so fierce that dare stir him up: who then is able to stand before me? Who hath prevented me, that I should repay him? whatsoever is under the whole heaven is mine" (Job 41:10–11). Although no person could stand before either leviathan or Satan, not even these could stand before the God of creation.

Job still knew little about the cosmic scientific experiment in which he had been the object tested, but he was gaining a much greater appreciation for and understanding of Almighty God than he had before his suffering. When made to realize the importance and majesty and purpose of the great creation, even his terrible sufferings became insignificant. And now God had revealed to his heart, even if he could not yet comprehend it fully in his mind, that there *had* been a purpose in his sufferings. They had not been inflicted because of his sins, as his "miserable comforters" had insisted, nor were they because God had abandoned him, as he had been tempted to believe. God's message revealed to him the vital importance of recognizing God as sovereign Creator in all things, of resting in that truth, and of leaving everything else up to him. The God of creation is also the God who loves and cares for his creation, and all who love and trust him in return can rejoice even in tribulations. Though Satan denied it, we *can* "serve God for nought," just because he is God!

Perhaps Job sensed the Satanic dimensions of his experience when God reminded him that even behemoth and leviathan (and, by extension, Satan himself) were his creatures and that he was well in control of the situation. God will allow suffering—even sin—for a season, for his own long-range purposes, but he "worketh all things after the counsel of his own will" (Eph. 1:11). God's plan of salvation is effective, as he demonstrated to Satan in the life of Job.

Job's suffering had another purpose, which Job could not have realized at the time. The day would come when he would record his experiences, as he had fervently desired to do (Job 19:23–24), and they would eventually be incorporated into the eternal Word of God, which had long ago been settled in heaven! (Ps. 119:89).

In this form, Job's testimony would be used as a challenge and a comfort to multitudes through the ages. In these last days, perhaps it can yet be used in an even greater way to call people back to the ultimate importance of creation and to the revealed Word and will of our sovereign Creator/ Redeemer.

Doom of the Dragon

Job knew much less in his day than we do today about "the wiles of the devil" (Eph. 6:11). We have the complete Bible, whereas all he had, at most, was the information now preserved in the early chapters of Genesis. He may have been able to discern a little more from God's veiled references to Satan as he described behemoth and leviathan, but he could hardly have known as much as we know about the meaning of his own experiences.

All those who accept a full creationist and inerrantist position on Scripture should now realize that the leviathan was what we call a dinosaur and what ancient people called a dragon. That leviathan also symbolizes Satan is evident from Isaiah 27:1. In the context of God's promised last-day judgment on the earth and its inhabitants, Isaiah prophesied: "In that day the LORD with his sore and great and strong sword shall punish leviathan the piercing serpent, even leviathan that crooked serpent; and he shall slay the dragon that is in the sea."

To foreshadow this end-time doom of Satan, God has already eliminated all real dragons from the earth. Scientists have long been mystified about the extinction of the giant dinosaurs and have proposed numerous theories. The one now in favor blames an asteroid bombardment at the close of the Cretaceous Period for the demise of dinosaurs, but this also has many difficulties. The catastrophe of the biblical flood, which left hordes of these creatures buried in future fossil graveyards all over the world, is a much more realistic explanation. The few that survived the flood— either on Noah's ark or in the flood waters—became extinct later due to climatological changes. In effect, God was promising this extinction to Job when he said that his "sword" could reach behemoth. He implied the same to Isaiah when he said his "strong sword" would punish leviathan. The psalms also noted: "Thou brakest the heads of the dragons in the waters. Thou brakest the heads of leviathan in pieces, and gavest him to be meat to the peoples inhabiting the wilderness" (Ps. 74:13–14). *dinosaur meat*

But the destruction of the dinosaur-dragons of the past is a type and prophecy of the final destruction of Satan in the future. This fearsome "king of all the children of pride" will be "brought down to hell" (Isa. 14:15).

As noted above, Satan was surely nearby in this final scene of the Book of Job, seeking desperately but unsuccessfully to destroy Job's faith and cause him to curse God. It is possible that he was present in the body of behemoth, as he had once used the body of the serpent in Eden, trying now to terrify suffering Job as a last, desperate resort. At the very least, he was symbolically present in God's description of the sea-monster, leviathan. Thus, although God was speaking to Job, he was also announcing his victory over Satan, both in the cosmic wager concerning Job and in the age-long spiritual conflict that would continue for another 5000 years. Satan may doubt it still, but his own doom, like that of the dinosaurs, is sure.

The dragon finally appears again in the last book of the Bible, not as the "angel of light" (2 Cor. 11:14), the guise in which he has deceived multitudes, but in his real nature, as the vicious dragon.

"And there was war in heaven: Michael and his angels fought against the dragon; and the dragon fought and his angels, And prevailed not; neither was their place found any more in heaven" (Rev. 12:7–8). No longer will Satan or any of his angels be able to enter God's presence in heaven to accuse the people of God, as he did against Job and as he continues to do in our day.

"And the great dragon was cast out, that old serpent, called the Devil, and Satan, which deceiveth the whole world: he was cast out into the earth, and his angels were cast out with him. And I heard a loud voice saying in heaven, Now is come salvation, and strength, and the kingdom of our God, and the power of his Christ: for the accuser of our brethren is cast down, which accused them before our God day and night" (Rev. 12:9–10).

Testing

This verse tells us that Satan accuses us as he did Job, and that God may allow him to test us, as he did Job. Christ allowed him to test Peter. "Simon, Simon, behold, Satan hath desired to have you, that he may sift you as wheat: But I have prayed for thee, that thy faith fail not: and when thou art converted, strengthen thy brethren" (Luke 22:31–32).

Satan may accuse us and try us, but the Lord Jesus Christ is our Defender! "If any man sin, we have an advocate with the Father, Jesus Christ the righteous; And he is the propitiation for our sins: and not for ours only, but also for the sins of the whole world" (1 John 2:1–2).

Finally all the testing will be over, and the great dragon will be destroyed. "And I saw an angel come down from heaven, having the key of the bottomless pit and a great chain in his hand. And he laid hold on the dragon, that old serpent, which is the Devil, and Satan, and bound him a thousand years, And cast him into the bottomless pit, and shut him up, and set a seal upon him, that he should deceive the nations no more" (Rev. 20:1–3).

This is not quite his final end, however. After the thousand-year reign of Christ and his saints over the earth, "he must be loosed a little season" (Rev. 20:3). After one final rebellion of men and devils, this conflict of the ages between God and Satan will be ended. "And the devil that deceived them was cast into the lake of fire and brimstone, . . . and shall be tormented day and night for ever and ever" (Rev. 20:10).

In that day, all the saints will learn, as Job did, that "the sufferings of this present time are not worthy to be compared with the glory which shall be revealed in us" (Rom. 8:18). We, like Job, will "have seen the end of the Lord; that the Lord is very pitiful, and of tender mercy" (James 5:11).

9

The End of the Lord

The final reference in the Bible to the patriarch Job is the beautiful testimony of James: "Take, my brethren, the prophets, who have spoken in the name of the Lord, for an example of suffering affliction, and of patience. Behold, we count them happy which endure. Ye have heard of the patience of Job, and have seen the end of the Lord; that the Lord is very pitiful, and of tender mercy" (James 5:10–11).

The Lord had not been callous or forgetful as he allowed Job to suffer such great affliction under the brutal onslaughts of Satan. The Lord is full of pity and tender mercy, and he knew that his servant would "endure," thus becoming for all later generations a marvelous example of patience and unwavering moral righteousness and personal faith in God.

Furthermore, the context in James implies that Job himself was one of "the prophets, who have spoken in the name of the Lord." This statement helps strengthen the case for Job as the original author of the book bearing his name. In the writings of a prophet, we can expect to find predictions about the coming Savior, which we do find in Job 19:25.

Confession and Deliverance

After the tremendous revelation he received of the glory of the Lord, of his great creation, and of God's loving care for his creation, Job no longer thought of his own problems. No longer did he plead for an understanding of his sufferings, or even seek relief from them. He had seen and heard the Lord, and nothing else was of any consequence.

When God finished his message of creation, climaxing it by asserting his power over mighty leviathan and implying final victory over sin, death, and Satan as well, Job had only one response. He humbly acknowledged God's omnipotence and omniscience and then confessed his own impotence and ignorance.

"I know that thou canst do every thing, and that no thought [device] can be withholden from thee" (Job 42:2). Job thought God had forgotten him, but finally realized that the God who created him even knew all his thoughts. Job may not have "sinned with his lips," but God knew his thoughts! Furthermore, God controls everything; nothing happens without his direct or indirect control. As the writer of Proverbs says: "The Lord hath made all things for himself: yea, even the wicked for the day of evil" (Prov. 16:4).

When we, like Job, see the magnitude and majesty of God as Creator, the infinite perfections of his creation, and the multitude of marvels by which he sustains his creation, our doubts and petty problems are easily resolved, and we simply trust him! We may not understand why God allows certain things, either in our own lives or in the lives of others, but we don't have to understand. God understands what he is doing with his own, and that is all that matters.

This is why Satan has labored so diligently over the centuries to supplant the knowledge of special creation and the omnipotence of God with the idea that "Nature" (i.e., evolu-

tion) accounts for the infinite complexities of the cosmos
and its creatures. Once men quit being God-centered in their
thoughts, they quickly become self-centered, and true worship of the Creator/Savior degenerates into pantheism, humanism, and eventually, at the end of the age, full-blown
Satanism.

Thus true biblical creationism is the answer to all human
needs and problems. This is the reason creation was the only
subject discussed by God when he responded to Job's desperate appeals.

Job confessed that he was unqualified to raise questions,
even in his mind, concerning God's dealings with men. Elihu
had darkened true counsel by speaking "words without
knowledge" (Job 38:2). Job admitted he had hidden "counsel
without knowledge" in his heart. He had even carelessly
spoken questions that were out of order, "things too wonderful for me." He had maintained strong faith in God despite severe afflictions and had steadfastly and truthfully
maintained his innocence of known sin, but when he saw the
Lord all his righteousness became less than nothing: "I have
heard of thee by the hearing of the ear: but now mine eye
seeth thee. Wherefore I abhor myself, and repent in dust and
ashes" (Job 42:5, 6).

The prophet Daniel, who was classed with Job and Noah
as one of the three most righteous men in history, had a
similar experience when he saw the Lord. "There remained
no strength in me: for my comeliness was turned into cor-
ruption, and I retained no strength" (Dan. 10:8).

John, the most beloved by Jesus of all his disciples, reac-
ted as follows when he saw him in his glory: "And when I
saw him, I fell at his feet as dead" (Rev. 1:17). When Job and
Daniel saw the Lord in his glory, they saw the pre-incarnate
Christ; when John saw him, he saw the glorified Christ, the
incarnate Word. "No man hath seen God at any time; the
only begotten Son, which is in the bosom of the Father, he
hath declared him" (John 1:18). Whenever and however the
infinite God has manifested himself to human eyes or ears, it

has been in the person of the Son, whose ministry it is to declare God to his creatures. Thus Job actually saw his redeemer, his daysman, while still in his suffering body. Surely it was a glorious sight beyond description. Job could only abhor himself, his questions, and even his own faith and upright life.

God, at this point, made his great announcement concerning the long dialogue between Job and his friends. Addressing Eliphaz and his two friends, God said: "My wrath is kindled against thee, and against thy two friends: for ye have not spoken of me the thing that is right, as my servant Job hath" (Job 42:7).

This statement is definitive as we seek to understand the lengthy discourses in chapters three through thirty-seven. Job had spoken truly concerning God, the others falsely. It is presumptuous, therefore, for those who would understand the book to seek other interpretations. Furthermore, God repeated his charge and required the three friends to offer sacrifices to atone for their sin of misrepresenting God: "Offer up for yourselves a burnt offering; and my servant Job shall pray for you: for him will I accept: lest I deal with you after your folly, in that ye have not spoken of me the thing which is right, like my servant Job" (Job 42:8).

It was not Job who had been trusting in his self-righteousness; it was his friends! They had been unable to accept the idea that their own comfort and prosperity were gifts of unmerited grace from their Maker and not God's reward for spirituality and morality. Consequently, they insisted against all evidence that Job was a wicked hypocrite whose suffering was God's punishment. Instead of bringing him the understanding and comfort he needed, they allowed themselves to be used by Satan to make Job's suffering even worse.

Elihu was not mentioned by God at this point, even though his attitude and accusations had been the same as those of the other three, made worse by his blasphemous assertion that he had received divine illumination to serve as God's messenger of rebuke to Job. It would seem, all things considered, that Elihu deserved at least as much rebuke as Eliphaz, Bildad, and Zophar. Perhaps God took his youth into account, attributing his arrogance to immaturity, impetuosity, and youthful pride, all of which would make him easy prey to demonic deception. Or, perhaps he had not yet been brought to repentance—as the other three friends apparently had been—and was unwilling to offer an atoning sacrifice or to ask Job to pray for him, still smug in his own self-righteousness and assumed spirituality.

In any case, God did not address Elihu directly, as he did the other three. Whatever his reason for ignoring him, he did not cause Job to record it for us, so we must leave it at that.

God did not require Job to offer a sacrifice, which is significant. Job had met this requirement long ago, and merely needed to confess once again his own unworthiness, acknowledging utter dependence upon his Creator/Redeemer. Eliphaz, Bildad, and Zophar offered seven bullocks and seven rams in Job's presence, as God required. The number seven has been a symbol of completeness since God's seventh-day rest after completing creation. Before God's revelations to Moses on Mount Sinai, seven may have been the number understood as appropriate for a comprehensive sacrifice to cover all sins in the nations that still believed in the God of creation. (This was the same sacrifice specified by the heretical prophet Balaam for the king of Moab. See Numbers 23:1, 29.)

Job did pray for his friends, forgiving them for their grievous slanders. God accepted his prayers, and their sacrifices, and forgave them as Job had. Such a forgiving attitude on Job's part after their bitter and unjust accusations provides further testimony to his godly character.

Finally, at long last, "the LORD turned the captivity of Job, when he prayed for his friends" (Job 42:10). This is God's way, as clearly taught by the Lord Jesus. "For if ye forgive men their trespasses, your heavenly Father will also forgive you: but if ye forgive not men their trespasses, neither will your Father forgive your trespasses" (Matt. 6:14–15).

Twice As Much

When the Lord "turned the captivity of Job," he not only healed and fully restored Job's dying body so he could live another 140 fruitful years, he also gave him double the prosperity he had known before. No doubt the news of God's amazing theophany and his clear vindication of "my servant Job," a phrase used four times to Job's friends (Job 42:7–8) and twice to Satan (Job 1:8; 2:3), quickly traveled through all the lands where Job had once been greatly revered.

Consequently, all his fair-weather friends and relatives (perhaps fearing that God might judge them even more harshly than he had Eliphaz, Bildad, and Zophar) came flocking back to honor Job and offer belated comfort. Furthermore, whether because of ancient custom or by God's command, each man "gave him a piece of money, and every one an earring of gold" (Job 42:11).

These gifts enabled Job to begin rebuilding his depleted flocks and herds, which eventually multiplied to the point that he was more prosperous than ever. "So the LORD blessed the latter end of Job more than his beginning: for he had fourteen thousand sheep, and six thousand camels, and a thousand yoke of oxen, and a thousand she asses" (Job 42:12).

This is exactly twice as much as Job had before he lost everything at the beginning of his troubles (see Job 1:3). Thus, "the LORD gave Job twice as much as he had before" (Job 42:10).

More important than the doubling of his possessions was the doubling of his family. His first family of seven sons and three daughters (Job 1:2, 17, 18) had died, but they were not really gone, as were his original flocks. His family had come to God through sacrifice and faith, as their father had taught them, and would be with him again some day.

After his restoration, Job eventually had another "seven sons and three daughters" (Job 42:13), a total of twenty children, all evidently faithful to God. Although the account does not say, it is probable that he also had a new wife. Job's first wife apparently abandoned him during his afflictions. She had urged her husband to "curse God, and die" (Job 2:9), and Job lamented later to his friends that "my breath is strange to my wife, though I intreated for the children's sake of mine own body" (Job 19:17). The loss of all her possessions and her children, and then her husband's terrible disfigurement, were probably more than she could bear.

After his restoration, Job lived another 140 years. His total age was probably 200 years or so, an age comparable to those of other godly patriarchs during that period (e.g., Abraham, 175 years; Terah, 205 years). Job had the joy of seeing all his great grandchildren grow up before he finally went to be with the Lord, whom he had served faithfully for so long.

Thus, Job's life, though filled with terrible privation and incredible suffering for one relatively short period of time, was capped off with a long period of peace, prosperity, and honor. This is suggestive of the great promise of 2 Corinthians 4:17: "For our light affliction, which is but for a moment, worketh for us a far more exceeding and eternal weight of glory." It also reminds us of "the sufferings of Christ, and the glory that should follow" (1 Peter 1:11).

We need to understand, however, that the happy ending of Job's story is not necessarily normative for the Christian believer in this age, except in its implied promise that our Creator/Redeemer will square accounts in the ages to come. In refuting his friends' claim that prosperity and peace are always the lot of the righteous, Job observed, "Wherefore do the wicked live, become old, yea, are mighty in power? . . . They spend their days in wealth, and in a moment go down to the grave" (Job 21:7, 13). There are many ungodly men who seem prosperous and happy all their days, and there are many godly and righteous men who suffer poverty and pain most of their lives. "One dieth in his full strength, being wholly at ease and quiet. . . . And another dieth in the bitterness of his soul, and never eateth with pleasure. They shall lie down alike in the dust, and the worms shall cover them" (Job 21:23–26).

Job's friends charged him with sin for uttering such words, but he spoke the truth, as confirmed by Christ himself: "Your Father. . .maketh his sun to rise on the evil and on the good, and sendeth rain on the just and on the unjust" (Matt. 5:45). Many faithful believers have suffered severely for the Lord: "They were stoned, they were sawn asunder, were tempted, were slain with the sword: they wandered about in sheepskins and goatskins; being destitute, afflicted, tormented; (Of whom the world was not worthy:) they wandered in deserts, and in mountains and in dens and caves of the earth. And these all, having obtained a good report through faith, received not the promise" (Heb. 11:37–39).

We are not to evaluate a person's spirituality by his prosperity. Paul calls people who make such judgments "men of corrupt minds, and destitute of the truth, supposing that gain is godliness: from such withdraw thyself" (1 Tim. 6:5). All such matters will be balanced out at the judgment seat of Christ (2 Cor. 5:10) and in the ages to come.

The return of Job's prosperity, therefore, should not be considered as an implied promise of prosperous happiness in this life. It is, instead, a testimony that "the end of the Lord," whether in this life or the life to come, is one that is "full of pity and tender mercy" (James 5:11). God, near the beginning of history, gave people in all ages this marvelous drama extolling his creation and his gracious sovereignty over all things, assuring us that he is fully aware and in full control, and that "all things work together for good to them that love God, to them who are the called according to his purpose" (Rom. 8:28).

Job and Christ

We have already noted some of Job's prophetic insights about the coming Savior. When Christ gave his disciples a Bible lesson on the Messianic prophecies, he began with Moses, who, as we have seen, was believed by the Jews of Jesus' day to be the author (or compiler and editor) of the

Book of Job. "Beginning at Moses and all the prophets, he expounded unto them in all the Scriptures the things concerning himself" (Luke 24:27). We should expect, therefore, to see the Lord Jesus Christ revealed in the pages of Job.

The specific references are not many, even though a Messianic spirit pervades the whole book. Probably the first is Job's famous query concerning the needed mediator. "For he is not a man, as I am, that I should answer him, and we should come together in judgment. Neither is there any daysman betwixt us, that might lay his hand upon us both" (Job 9:32–33).

Job expressed here the great need for one who was both God and man, who could "lay his hand upon us both." The great need of lost men and women, separated by sin from their Creator, is for an arbitrator, called a daysman in earlier times. God had long ago promised that "the seed of the woman" (that is, a man) would destroy the serpent (a task to which only God was equal). This protevangelic promise of Genesis 3:15 thus anticipated a coming God/man, the very need expressed here by Job and finally fulfilled in Christ. "For there is one God, and one mediator between God and men, the man Christ Jesus" (1 Tim. 2:5).

Then we have Job's great statement of faith: "Though he slay me, yet will I trust in him: but I will maintain mine own ways before him. He also shall be my salvation: for an hypocrite shall not come before him" (Job 13:15–16). The word translated *salvation* here is the Hebrew *yeshua* (meaning Jehovah saves), and is nothing less than the name *Jesus*. Thus an ancient Jew would read this passage as follows: "...yet will I trust in him:... He also shall be my Jesus!" Job and other godly men of old, in or out of Israel, would have known that salvation could come only from Jehovah through the promised God/man, the most appropriate name for whom would be *Yeshua*, or Jesus, and that they must trust him to be saved.

Undoubtedly the greatest Messianic prophecy in Job—in fact, one of the greatest in the Bible—is his cry: "For I know that my redeemer liveth, and that he shall stand at the latter day upon the earth: And though after my skin worms destroy this body, yet in my flesh shall I see God: Whom I shall see for myself, and mine eyes shall behold, and not another; though my reins be consumed within me" (Job 19:25–27).

Surely this was a divinely inspired revelation. Job recognized that his desired mediator must also be his Redeemer. To bridge the gulf between man and God, the God/man could only become his Savior if he could pay the ransom to buy him back from the slave-master of sin and death. This must involve the substitutionary death (for *that* is the price!) of the Redeemer, but then he must also rise from the dead to complete the work of redemption. Job could see that his Redeemer must live, and that he also would be raised from the dead in the latter day, not just in the spirit, for he would see God (his Redeemer is also the Creator!) in his flesh. What a tremendous truth and gracious promise from our mighty Creator/Mediator/Redeemer/Savior, appropriated by Job 4000 years ago and even more personally real to us today!

In addition to such explicit prophecies of the coming Savior, there is an important sense in which Job himself is a beautiful type of Christ. His narrative serves as a prophetic foreshadowing of Christ's experiences in becoming our Savior. We cannot be dogmatic about this, since the New Testament never identifies Job as a specific type of Christ, but the parallels are so striking that they seem to have been intended.

The first verse of Job identifies him as a man "perfect and upright, and one that feared God, and eschewed evil" (Job 1:1). As such, he was surely as ideal a human type as could be found for "Jesus Christ the righteous," for "in him is no sin" (1 John 2:1; 3:5). The account of Job opens with the introduction of Satan trying to tempt Job to renounce God. Similarly, the public ministry of Christ began with his experience of testing by the wicked one. "And immediately the Spirit driveth him into the wilderness. And he was there in the wilderness forty days, tempted of Satan; and was with the wild beasts; and the angels ministered unto him" (Mark 1:12–13). Just as the angels of God came to Christ after Satan tempted him, God himself came to rescue his servant Job. In both cases, Satan was defeated: Job retained his integrity and his faith; and Jesus, in his humanity, resisted every temptation Satan could devise to make him abandon his submission to the Father.

During the time of his humiliation, when he "was made in the likeness of men" (Phil. 2:7), Jesus had the sad experience of having his own human family reject him: "for neither did his brethren believe in him" (John 7:5). One of the Messianic psalms put it this way: "I am become a stranger unto my brethren, and an alien unto my mother's children. For the zeal of thine house hath eaten me up; and the reproaches of them that reproached thee are fallen upon me" (Ps. 69:8–9). Similarly, note Job's testimony: "He hath put my brethren far from me, and mine acquaintance are verily estranged from me. My kinsfolk have failed, and my familiar friends have forgotten me" (Job 19:13–14). In both cases, however, their families and friends returned to full fellowship with them after their periods of suffering had ended.

Job's humiliation required the loss of all his extensive possessions. Jesus, likewise, "though he was rich, yet for your sakes he became poor" (2 Cor. 8:9), and when he died, even the clothing he wore was taken from him.

Job also endured terrible physical suffering. The following complaints from Job sound almost like Messianic prophecies: "They have gaped upon me with their mouth; they have smitten me upon the cheek reproachfully; they have gathered themselves together against me. God hath delivered me to the ungodly, and turned me over into the hands of the wicked" (Job 16:10–11). "They abhor me, they flee far from me, and spare not to spit in my face. . . . And now my soul is poured out upon me; the days of affliction have taken hold upon me. My bones are pierced in me in the night season: and my sinews take no rest" (Job 30:10, 16–17).

Compare these with the following undisputed Messianic prophecies, all explicitly fulfilled in the sufferings of Christ:

"All they that see me laugh me to scorn:... they shake the head, saying, He trusted on the LORD that he would deliver him: let him deliver him, seeing he delighted in him.... I am poured out like water, and all my bones are out of joint:... For dogs have compassed me: the assembly of the wicked have inclosed me: they pierced my hands and my feet" (Ps. 22:7-8, 14, 16); "I gave my back to the smiters, and my cheeks to them that plucked off the hair: I hid not my face from shame and spitting" (Isa. 50:6). These and other similar descriptions seem to apply equally well to the sufferings of either Jesus or Job.

Job's sufferings were so traumatic that he thought God had forsaken him. His friends rebuked him for this attitude, and so have many expositors. We need to remember, however, that the Lord Jesus himself, in his human suffering on the cross, also cried out: "My God, my God, why hast thou forsaken me?" (Matt. 27:46). The intriguing paradox here is that God apparently had forsaken Job though he was the most righteous of all men, but he apparently forsook Christ because he was being made sin for all men.

In the case of the Lord Jesus Christ, his sufferings and apparent abandonment by the Father culminated in death. Job could not die, because his survival was part of the terms of the heavenly wager. But Job desired to die, and indeed knew his sufferings would culminate in death if God did not intervene: "For I know that thou wilt bring me to death," he said, near the end of his last discourse (Job 30:23).

Finally, Job was delivered from his sufferings and restored, not only to his former position of prosperity and honor, but "the LORD blessed the latter end of Job more than his beginning" (Job 42:12).

Still more glorious is the latter end of the Lord Jesus Christ, even as his righteousness was more perfect than Job's, his humiliation more extreme, his conflict with Satan more intense, and his sufferings more severe. Job, in many respects, is a beautiful type of Christ, but he was only a type—the reality is Christ himself! Job's sufferings were imposed without his knowledge and understanding, but Christ willingly accepted his in full knowledge of the hellish depths to which they would reach.

There is no greater testimony of the incomparable scope of God's grace than in the contrast between his glory as Creator and his lonely, bitter humiliation as sin-bearing Savior. This central theme of the ages was foreshadowed in the humiliation of the great patriarch Job and in his eventual exaltation, not only to his former position but even to the mediating ministry of intercession for others. The great truth which it prefigured is expressed most powerfully and beautifully in the famous *kenosis* (emptying) passage in Philippians, and this is a fitting testimony with which to conclude this exposition.

> Let this mind be in you, which was also in Christ Jesus: Who, being in the form of God, thought it not robbery to be equal with God: but made himself of no reputation, and took upon him the form of a servant, and was made in the likeness of men: And being found in fashion as a man, he humbled himself, and became obedient unto death, even the death of the cross.
>
> Wherefore God also hath highly exalted him, and given him a name which is above every name: That at the name of Jesus every knee should bow, of things in heaven, and things in earth, and things under the earth; And that every tongue should confess that Jesus Christ is Lord, to the glory of God the Father (Phil. 2:5–11).

Collateral damage

transparent impenetrability

Subject Index

140

Scripture Index